FOIL

Random House  New York

CHARLES A. SELBERG *University of California, Santa Cruz*

FOIL

First Edition
9876

ISBN: 0-394-34896-6

Manufactured in the United States of America

PREFACE

Twenty-five years ago one could rarely find fencing instruction offered through regularly scheduled courses in our public schools and colleges. Fencing was regarded as a "European sport," receiving little public support. Its image in the United States was anachronistic and romantic. The Hollywood version of swashbuckling swordplay presented fencing as aristocratic and theatrical, creating the popular impression that fencing did not belong to the twentieth century. Few people are aware that fencing was and is a modern Olympic sport.

Fencing in the United States depended for its existence on a handful of private clubs and schools which were fortunate enough to have European-trained Fencing Masters.

Since then, American fencing has experienced a startling growth in popularity. Twenty-five years ago San Francisco State, Stanford University, and the University of California at Berkeley comprised the total membership of the Northern California Intercollegiate Fencing Association. Today the same association includes seventeen member colleges. This same acceleration of fencing activity can be observed throughout the United States. It is not surprising to discover that the majority of young fencers today receive their training in our high schools, community colleges, colleges, and universities. This stands in sharp contrast to twenty-five years ago, when the majority of fencers were trained in the private fencing club. Fencing is no longer regarded as a strictly European sport, but rather has taken its proper place within the context of American physical education. Physical education now recognizes fencing within its list of lifetime sports.

This transformation has created a pressing need for more fencing teachers. Subsequently, we now observe American trained fencers and physical education teachers drawn by the enthusiasm of the young into the task of teaching fencing, which itself has undergone many changes over the last few years. Students and teachers alike who find themselves confronted with the complexities of learning, updating, teaching, and coaching modern foil should find this book of value.

The material presented in the following chapters is drawn from both my reading of the many books available on fencing, and my own competitive experience, which extends intensively over a twenty-year period. As one who has taught and coached fencing on all levels during the past fifteen years, it is my hope that the practical experience I have gained in this capacity may lend useful insights to the reader.

It is not my intention to present material which is original or new to the fencing world, but rather to offer a first-rate reference relating to basic modern foil fencing which is simplified, relatively comprehensive, and understandable to both the beginning and advanced levels of fencing interest. If there is an innovative note in my approach, it exists in the relatively in-depth treatment I have given the material in an effort to integrate the technical, tactical, and psychological ingredients of good fencing.

During the early years of my own fencing development, instruction frequently was directed toward the purely technical aspects of fencing skill. It was not until I had the good fortune to study under the late George Piller that I came to understand that the rationale behind a given action is as important to the fencer as the action itself. The fencer who understands why a particular technique takes shape will seldom be at a loss to know *when* and *how* to use it to best advantage. The fencer, especially the beginner, must know the full implications of basic technique if he or she is to be aware of its potential as well as its limitations. It is with this in mind that special emphasis is given in this format to those underlying principles of physical and mental balance which give meaning and shape to fencing technique.

I have included useful information relating to tactics and the psychological elements of competitive fencing. Little has been written on this crucial aspect of fencing; and while the material will be most meaningful to those with competitive experience, beginners will find it directly related to their own situations. This is perhaps the most interesting and complex part of fencing. One could say that these tactical and psychological elements *are* fencing, for without the ability to think and respond creatively to the demands of the serious competitor, technique becomes the surest path to frustration and futility. The mental processes of the fencer must be in tune with the lightning-fast aggressive demands of his or her adversary. While acknowledging that no two fencers ever fence alike, it becomes clear that tactics and psychology are at the core of an effective game. It has been my observation over the years that the tactics and psychology of fencing are the most difficult areas of instruction and fencing preparation.

Finally, the technical material presented in this book does not advocate one style of fencing over another. Each fencer must ultimately build a game based on his or her own best assets and predispositions. It is my primary intention to present material which is universal to all good fencing styles and which will aid anyone in the development of a game that can function effectively within the context of modern standard or electrical foil fencing. This material should lead the reader to a better understanding of his or her own game as well as that of his or her opponents. It is assumed that the technique, strategy, and psychology of modern fencing serve only as material whereby each fencer may build his or her own unique and individual style as a means to high-level performance.

In my own development as a fencer I studied under four Fencing Masters, each of whom emphasized different approaches to the game. One placed importance on perfect technical execution while another emphasized the need for flowing rhythmic movement and timing. The third stressed powerful physical conditioning coupled with controlled aggression, while the fourth placed prime importance on strategy and psychological advantage. Each of these teachers viewed fencing in his own way and developed strong fencers through his individual method. Each of them contributed an essential ingredient to my game for which I am most grateful.

But more than this, I learned that no two teachers teach alike or agree completely on which approach is best. I have tried in this book to include the advantages of all styles of fencing, concentrating on the essentials that each has in common. If you are on the path into the stimulating and fascinating world of fencing, this book may be used as one more stepping stone toward a most challenging goal.

Santa Cruz, California   C.A.S.
September 1975

ACKNOWLEDGMENTS

In a very real sense, fencers who have contributed to my understanding of and interest in fencing over a period of years are responsible for the creation of this book. Special thanks must be given to the many students with whom I have been associated, who through their curiosity, questions, and observations have extended my own understanding of fencing. While it is impossible to list everyone, I wish to acknowledge Lance King, Paul Dart, Peter Ashley, Kate and Richard Simpson, Christopher Dworin, Nancy McMurtry, John Watanabe, James Bubar, Howard Gong, Richard Hill, John Maenchen, Dr. Blaine Amidon and Diana, Julie Moore Selberg, Nicholas Follansbee, and the redoubtable Lance Bayer.

Also, I must express a genuine indebtedness to the Northern California Division of the Amateur Fencers League of America, where I gained my primary fencing education in practical circumstances, where I competed against the finest group of sportsmen I have been privileged to know, who have always acted as a reality check to my thinking. On the East Coast I am particularly indebted to Maitres Raoul Sudre and Jean Jacques Gillet of Cornell University, Edwin Richards of the Massachusetts Institute of Technology, and Chaba Elthes of the New York Fencer's Club, through whose association and friendship I have gained invaluable insights to the theory and practice of fencing.

Grateful appreciation is given to the University of California at Santa Cruz, where, through an enlightened approach to physical education, I have been given ample opportunity to put into practice the theories and recommendations presented in this book.

For the photographic efforts included in this format, thanks go to John McDougall, Alan Donaldson, Bernie Guzenski, Michael Bellar, and Jan Meyerson. Also, grateful appreciation must be extended to Miss Gay Jacobsen, 1974 Women's United States National Foil champion, for appearing in several of these pictures along with her coach, Michael Dasaro.

Important aspects of this text are a by-product of discussion between myself and Michael Dasaro, Fencing Master at San Jose State University, where together we have explored new approaches to an understanding of modern fencing. The vast teaching and competitive experience that Mr. Dasaro brought to his reading of several chapters in this text proved most valuable.

Appreciation is extended to Jean Helliwell of Stanford University and Fencing Master Julius Palffy-Alpar of the University of California at Berkeley; through my association with Ms. Helliwell and Mr. Alpar I have gained valuable insights into teaching and coaching. Their knowledge and enthusiasm for fencing has acted as an inspiration through many passages of this book.

I wish to acknowledge the late Masters Eric Funke, Hans Halberstadt, Aldo Nadi, and George Piller, all of whom were instrumental in my development as a teacher of fencing and whose influence still reflects itself in my approach to fencing methodology.

I would be remiss if mention were not made of Bill Snyder, John McDonough, Norman Selberg, and Mary Holmes, whose example and encouragement have always taken me over rough times when creative energy was low.

Marcia Wiesner has proved most helpful through her editorial and typing efforts, coupled with an unending patience which was most helpful in bringing this manuscript into completed form.

The permission granted by the Amateur Fencer's League of America to reproduce the rules of right-of-way as they are presented in this format is greatly appreciated.

Finally, with a text of this nature it would be impossible to cover all material which relates to fencing. If there are mistakes or omissions in this text they are solely the responsibility of the writer.

Miss Gay Jacobsen, nineteen-year-old 1974 United States Women's National Champion. Miss Jacobsen attends San Jose State University, where she trains under Fencing Master Michael Dasaro.

THE NATURE OF FENCING

by John M. Watanabe

Romantic intellectualism—what else can fencing be called? The intense concentration, the precise control, the flash of inspired creativity— fencing demands all these acts of intellection, intellection in the true sense of the word: the exercise of the power of knowing. Fencing has its background in the Old World aristocratic tradition: the white uniform, the sword, the duel of honor. But the overly romantic dreams of an aspiring D'Artagnon or Cyrano de Bergerac have no place in modern fencing, and indeed, few serious fencers entertain such fantasies.

You stand in the center of a strip six feet wide and some fifty feet long, dressed from head to foot in a white uniform. Your gloved hand holds the foil lightly between the fingertips and the heel of the palm, and under your other arm you hold a steel mesh mask—your protection from an ill-aimed thrust to the face or eyes. Your adversary stands across from you, similarly attired. You salute each other, a simple rais- ing of the foil vertically in front of the face which concludes with a swift downsweep of the blade to the right. You then put on your mask and step into the guard position, knees flexed, body upright, the unarmed hand raised above the shoulder.

You move with the two-tempo beat of the advance and the retreat, engaging your opponent's blade, beating lightly on it, testing his or her defenses, and waiting. An opening presents itself and you react instinc- tively—there is no time for thought or plan, you know what to do and you do it instantaneously. If the attack is properly timed and executed, your blade bends on your opponent's chest while his or her own blade is flailing in ineffectual attempts to stem your irresistible attack. But your slightest hesitation or misjudgment seals your own doom in the clash of a parried attack which is followed by your opponent's immediate and equally unstoppable counterattack.

Such is fencing at its best.

Fencing is a vastly simplified reflection of the larger world, and through this simplification your sense of perception and knowledge and the way you interact with other human beings can be clarified. Fencing is a world of actions uncluttered by spoken words; communication is through action, and action is knowledge. Words can be used to express "knowing what" fencing is, but they are utterly useless in "knowing how" to go about fencing. Fencing knowledge, like all knowledge, is active creativity—a creativity which can only be experienced, not taught.

While fencing is in one sense a physical skill with mechanical aspects which must be learned, it is basically a *creative* process. The mastery of fencing's mechanical techniques, such as how to move, how to parry, how to attack, results by no means in the mastery of the sport itself. A technically perfect fencer with no imagination or creativity in his or her game is a fencer without soul. The knowledge of this fencer is the knowledge of the taker—the calculating perfectionism of a low-risk opportunist.

Conversely, the insensitive fencer who disregards all technique—who is all creativity—is another kind of taker, enclosed in a private, ego-centered world of self-assertive independence. He or she needs nothing but the freedom to satisfy his or her own wants and desires. Both of these kinds of fencers—the technical perfectionist and the assertive individualist—are unwilling to change or give up an old part of themselves in order to gain something new. Neither can understand that the acquisition of knowledge is a risk of one's own self-esteem.

True fencers recognize this element of risk and accept the fact that they can never excel in fencing until they gain control of their desire to *possess* every bit of fencing knowledge. Fencing at its best is a *state of mind* based on—but not limited by—certain fundamental techniques. There is no room for desire or possessiveness. Indeed, true fencers realize that one can never know a parry or an attack in or by itself. Knowledge comes only at the instant of execution—with the feeling of discovery that comes with the conviction of instantaneous comprehension through experience. Knowledge as action is creative, not mechanical; it is adaptive, not specific.

A large part of fencing skill involves perception—perception of not only one's own actions and reactions, but of these same processes in the opponent. True fencing can take place only when a fencer *acts with*, rather than *reacts to*, the adversary. Thus, fencing demands an empathy with one's opponent—not so much the entering into the other's experience as the realization that that other experience exists.

There is no judgment involved in a fencing bout. The creativity, the *pouring out* of a fencer's skill does not demand—indeed, it is destroyed by—critical judgment. You cannot judge an opponent and fence him or her at the same time. There can only be an attitude of *acritical perception* or empathy in the true fencer. This empathy cannot be asserted, it can only be experienced. The moment you *try* to perceive your opponent's next action, you become a reactor—or at best a calculating planner. Then creativity disappears, and your own preconceptions effectively block out any true awareness of your opponent. Fencing becomes a mechanical guessing game, a critical judgment of everyone's ability but your own.

Stereotype, preconception, and desire have no place in the truly skillful fencer. Fencing skill is the epitome of willing without being willful, of experiencing knowledge without asserting it. It is only when you can perceive acritically—listening and seeing without that inner dialogue and judgment which has become such an integral part of our interaction with other people—that fencing truly becomes knowledge as action. Only then can you make the total commitment which real learning demands. There is no concern for perfectionism or evaluation, only the appreciation of experience—the split-second elation of "yes, that's it!" which comes with the right action.

The fencing master can lead you, the student, only so far. Once the master has demonstrated the basic techniques, it is up to you to give these techniques the life and creativity necessary for skillful fencing. The master serves as your example of a higher level of knowledge—of an awareness beyond your own experience. Only through the perception and attempted understanding of this higher awareness do you gradually learn and grow. The master cannot eliminate the risk, the discouragement, or the frustration of the change which new knowledge demands, but he can show you from what direction the change must come. His is the authoritative voice of balanced praise and criticism which you cannot supply from within yourself.

You must possess confidence in your own ability, tempered with the realization that knowledge does not fall magically from the hand of your teacher. True learning is a difficult process, a total commitment to the discovery of new and unexpected insights and experiences. It is an acritical look deep into the self—the revelation of something so right it seems you knew it all along. Only the combination of this commitment on the part of the student and the authoritative—yet not authoritarian—voice of the master can create the knowledgeable, skillful fencer.

Sensitivity and balance must always be maintained. To strive toward anything else is to learn nothing at all. Self-confidence must be balanced with humility, for only with humility may one still the inner dialogue—the constant desire of self-assertion—and open the way for true learning.

Fencing is the epitome of serious playfulness. When you don your fencing mask, you enter a realm entirely separate from the larger world. The intensity of concentration, the creativity, the pouring out of yourself experienced in a fencing bout resembles the seriousness of a child at play. Playing is an attitude, not an activity; it is a freedom and creativity that comes from the courage of complete commitment. There is no calculation in play, only a richness of experience.

One needs no justification for a love of fencing; one does it because it is enjoyable. This is not to say that it is always pleasant. It is not. Often it is discouraging, frustrating, or just plain exhausting. But there are also moments of total commitment, vivid perception, and, very rarely, the exhilaration of true knowledge in the proper execution of an attack or parry. The real joy of fencing is not *mastery*—mastery of a skill, a mastery of an opponent, or even mastery of oneself—but it is the elation of *knowledge as action*, of a skill which has only a transient reality in the motion, speed, timing, and accuracy of an extremely simple—but infinitely difficult—action.

CONTENTS

CHAPTER 1

THE SWORD, PAST AND PRESENT

EARLY HISTORY

Fencing finds its origins in a far distant, brutal, and sometimes colorful past. Unlike many sports, fencing was born out of a grim reality that bears little resemblance to the sophisticated sport we enjoy today. While the modern electric game identifies only slightly with the dueling practices of the Renaissance, or the brutish arena encounters of the Romans, it must be observed that fencing has its antecedents in the encounters of antiquity and the dueling codes of Europe. It is interesting to speculate on the effect the sword has had in shaping culture, for one can trace a clear evolution of hand weapons and "swordplay" from the earliest societies to the present.

EVOLUTION OF HAND WEAPONRY

The sword has undergone a startling evolution over a period of four thousand years. In essence, heavy and unwieldy weapons of earlier times were transformed, through necessity, into the light precision fencing instruments used today. This gradual transformation was effected by improved methods in metallurgy, creating a weapon which is strong, light, and fast.

1

The earliest Egyptian swords were made of copper or bronze. They were cumbersome and short, due to the excessive quantity of soft metal necessary for the construction of a blade that could resist bending and breaking. The copper sword was too heavy for efficient use, requiring the swordsman to employ it more as a metal club than as a cutting instrument. With the advent of iron blades the copper weapon became obsolete. Copper was simply no match for iron.

By the time of the Greek and Roman civilizations, iron weapons were used exclusively and were constructed essentially along the lines of the earlier copper prototypes. The highest development in this form

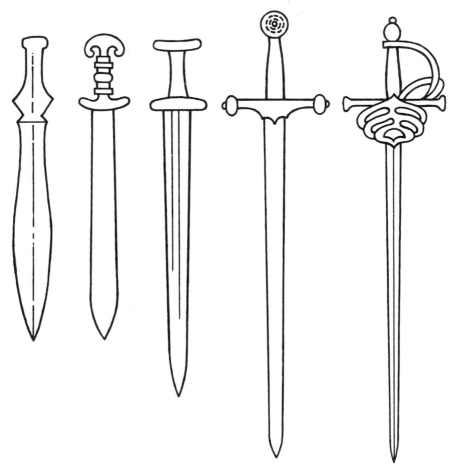

Fig. 1.1. Early swords; left to right: Egyptian, Roman, Viking, crusader, Spanish Renaissance triangular steel blade.

of iron sword was the Roman "short sword," which was, at best, a crude fighting instrument compared with innovations yet to come in the form of steel.

THE DUELING SWORD

European cultures inherited the steel blade from the Vikings, who terrorized the coastal and river regions of Europe through the eighth, ninth, and tenth centuries. The Viking sword was to instigate a revolution in the design of hand weaponry and create new fighting techniques throughout Europe.

The use of steel created a longer, stronger, and lighter weapon which could be used for thrusting. In effect, the short, heavy weapons of past ages, which were suited primarily for hacking, were replaced by long, pointed steel blades, which were not only better equipped for hacking, but also had the advantage of the thrust. This change was the first evidence that versatility could dominate over the brute strength tactics of past swordsmen. In many respects the steel thrusting weapon opened the door to modern fencing.

The Vikings and Germanic tribes of Northern Europe contributed a veneration of the sword to European society. The sword became a symbol of knighthood and justice in the Middle Ages and was used to settle legal disputes in the form of the "judicial duel." The conventions governing this formalized combat are perhaps the first manifestation of "rules of play" for fencing in Western society. Many forms of dueling evolved from the judicial duel, including the "chivalrous duel," which started during the eleventh century, and the "duel of honor," beginning in the fifteenth century.[1] Dueling created a need to codify the conventions of swordfighting, resulting in the production of written materials and schools of fencing. The fifteenth century gave rise to the first fencing school in Spain, with the French, Italians, and Germans following suit in the sixteenth century.

Paralleling the rise of schools of combat for dueling, improvements in steel making led to better forms of weaponry. The Spanish created the triangular steel blade, which was extremely light, maneuverable, and strong. This is the prototype of modern thrusting weapons. The lightness and thrusting strength of the Spanish blade caused "swordplay" to be faster and deadlier. By the sixteenth century, dueling found its total strength in dexterity and mental adroitness, which placed a premium on strategy and tactics. The swordsman could no longer depend on physical strength and endurance for survival. Skill was now a factor. The light, fast blade, coupled with intelligent use of tactical and technical advantage, was the key to success from the sixteenth century onward.

The mechanics of the duel were as fascinating and as complex as chess, because intelligence had become a basic ingredient for success. It was only natural that the social form of the duel would eventually become a sport. By the eighteenth century protective equipment had been created which brought swordsmanship from the dueling ground into the sporting arena. The invention of the wire-mesh mask and the blunt-tipped foil made it possible to engage in swordplay without the risk of injury. This, then, is the basic difference between fencing and dueling, which involves bloodshed. By the eighteenth century dueling had been outlawed throughout Europe because of the thousands of fatalities which occurred through its practice.[2] With the end of dueling, fencing was to gain wide popularity as a form of sport which would eventually be recognized as suitable for Olympic and world competition.

FRENCH AND ITALIAN TECHNIQUES

Of the many schools of fencing, the French and Italian have proved superior. These two great schools of fencing vied with each other for dominance well into the twentieth century. A proper understanding of the differences between the French and Italian techniques is essential to a comprehension of modern electrical fencing. The essential differences must be generalized, for each technique contains a good deal of the other. Traditionally, the Italian technique was one of athletic emphasis, while the French placed prime value on the mental aspects of the encounter. The Italian technique presents explosive offensive power unlike the French style, which depends on intellectual defensive strategy. The athletic discipline of Italian fencing and its intuitive faith in the attack as a means of scoring stand traditionally in contrast to the French game, which takes pride in defensive strategy, depending on the riposte for its primary means of delivering the touch. Temperamentally, each school found itself at variance with the other, reflecting cultural predisposition in its technical approach. It is interesting to note that neither Italian power nor French finesse could demonstrate a clear superiority over a period of centuries. Each school had its share of great fencing masters: men like Greco, Pini, Persina, and Nadi in Italy; and Kirchoffer, Mirignac, Rue, and Gaudin in France.[3]

Fig. 1.2. Hans Halberstadt (1883–1966), second from the left, was one of the first European-trained Fencing Masters to introduce fencing to the San Francisco Bay area.

MODERN FOIL

When international fencing competition resumed after the termination of World War II, a general melding of French and Italian techniques could be observed in world competition. The overt signs of a new synthesis of techniques were rapidly becoming the rule rather than the exception among the best fencers in Europe. The Russians, who had taken a serious interest in fencing during this period, were instrumental in codifying this synthesis. Russian Fencing Masters, having little fencing tradition to prejudice their thinking, pragmatically combined elements of French and Italian techniques with the intrinsic potential of the electrical foil, which was adopted for official world competition in 1957. They created a new formalized fencing methodology which now dominates world competitive events and has given birth to a truly modern foil game.

Fig. 1.3. Hans Halberstadt in his salle on Fillmore Street, San Francisco in 1943.

Electric Foil

The most recent technical influence on the evolution of fencing is found in the electrical scoring device. Electrical fencing has placed demands on fencing that we are still bringing into focus. The electrical foil has modified and reshaped the older styles of fencing and has opened a new range of speculation relating to tactics and conditioning. The modern fencer is no longer dependent on the jury system of the "standard" or nonelectric game, which demanded visual proof of each touch. Where the touch was essentially defined as "one seen by the jury," it is now defined electrically as a touch that "arrives." The implication is that now the fencer can score *faster than visual perception*, confident that every valid touch will be recorded. The superior pace of electrical fencing could not avoid creating modifications in fencing techniques which were geared to the "standard" visual game.

   The classic heritage of the French and Italian systems is giving way to a new perception of fencing. Fencing has acquired a new aesthetic consciousness which has emerged from the context of electrical methodology and portends a continued evolutionary process in fencing technique. [4]

FENCING AND ITS ORGANIZATION

The A.F.L.A.

The Amateur Fencers' League of America (A.F.L.A.) was founded in 1891 in response to the growth of fencing interest in the United States. The A.F.L.A. is the official governing body for fencing throughout the United States. It is recognized by the United States Olympic Committee, the National Collegiate Athletic Association, the National Fencing Coaches' Association and the Federation d'Escrime, which establishes rules and regulations governing the conduct of fencing competition throughout the world.

All A.F.L.A. competition is organized along divisional and regional lines, culminating in the United States National Championships which are held each year. It is through A.F.L.A. competitive events that the fencer may earn points toward eligibility for the United States Olympic and World Championship teams.

A.F.L.A. membership is available to all persons interested in fencing. Members may receive the Official Rules book published by the A.F.L.A. and a subscription to *American Fencing* magazine, which is published bi-monthly. The provisions of the Rules book are mandatory for all championship and nationally rated competitions. All officers of the A.F.L.A. are elected by the membership and receive no financial compensation.

Fencing centers. Primary centers for fencing in the United States are New York and surrounding environs, Los Angeles, San Francisco, Chicago, and Detroit. While fencing activity exists throughout the United States, it is in the large urban centers, where universities, colleges, and private fencing clubs attract students, that one finds the liveliest interest in the sport.

REFERENCES

1. Robert Baldick, *The Duel—A History of Dueling*. New York: Clarkson N. Potter, Inc., 1965.
2. Francis Bacon, *The Charge Touching Duels*. New York: Da Capo Press, 1968.
3. Julio Martinez Castillo, *The Theory and Practice of Fencing*. New York-London: Charles Scribner's Sons, 1933, p. 5.
4. For a comprehensive discussion and analysis of the new electric foil aesthetic, read Istvan Lukovich, *Electric Foil Fencing*, New York: Corvina Press, 1971.

CHAPTER 2

FENCING, FACTS AND MYTHS

TECHNICAL TERMS

Because fencing has its roots in a European sports context, a number of technical terms from the French and Italian languages, which have no English counterparts, must be employed. The conscientious fencer must give careful attention to terms of this nature, ensuring that definitions and connotations are clearly understood. This aspect of fencing is frequently overlooked, creating long-range difficulties for the student which are reflected by insecure tactics and poor technical application. Terms such as "remise," "reprise," "riposte," "tempo," "pattinando," and "ballestra" are often only vaguely understood. This material, studied properly, will always add clarity and strength to one's game.

MOTIVATION

Because fencing is a nontraditional American sport which is seldom given exposure through the mass media, the majority of students who enroll for beginning fencing have virtually no conception of what fencing is. Adding insult to injury, many appear for their first instruction expecting fencing to somehow reflect the dramatic excitement of swashbuckling movies, romantic literature, or Shakespearean drama. Another popular assumption is that fencing is an art form, associated with dance.

Whether the individual is motivated to fencing out of pure curiosity or for other reasons, his or her first task is one of clarifying the nature of the game before technical instruction begins. The student who possesses an accurate conception of the nature of fencing will be motivated by a desire to learn the "real thing." Otherwise, the student runs the risk of experiencing disillusionment and frustration later, when the discovery is made that fencing isn't at all what had been expected. Correct understanding ensures interest.

THE SPORT OF FENCING

Fencing must be learned as a sport. The reason people fence is no different from the motivation behind golf, tennis, handball, or any other sport. Fencing is an athletic pastime in which one can participate either competitively or recreationally. Fencing offers an exciting, pleasurable, and healthful means of recreation. For the student, fencing is an exceptionally fine release from the sedentary nature of academic life. A few hours of fencing per week will keep the body trim and the mind alert. There is no need to defend the advantages of physical activity; and fencing offers a most interesting athletic outlet for anyone seeking vigorous exercise.

Intrinsic Values of Fencing

Every sport possesses its own intrinsic nature. Fencing is no exception, offering unique challenges to all who participate. Instruction relates directly to techniques of relaxation, control of energy and mental disposition, hand-eye coordination, physical movement, fighting psychology, and mind-body harmony. There is no physical prerequisite for skilled fencing other than a healthy body, which may be acquired in the process of learning to fence. There is no advantage in being short or tall. Fencing demands only that individuals discover their own best assets and learn to use them constructively. As the only Western "martial art," fencing enjoys a unique place among American sports.

Fencing is perfectly suited to both men and women. Men and women love to fence each other, which is unique among competitive sports. Fencing should always be programmed as co-recreational in our schools.

It is impossible to learn fencing from only a book. While a good fencing book can be an excellent source of new ideas, supplementary material, and fresh perspective, the student of fencing must learn the basic skills on a "first-hand" basis, from another fencer or teacher. The basic techniques of fencing cannot be presented or learned academically or through photographs. As in all sports, the fundamental basis of technique has no counterpart outside of *space, movement,* and *touch.* For this, the fencing student must have practical experience somewhere in his or her background. This point is easily misunderstood. I have observed many students who tried to learn fencing with a text as their only frame of reference. They soon came to understand that the situation they faced was impossible and either abandoned the effort completely or rushed off to the nearest fencing instructor to correct their circumstances.

The following is a list of *basic techniques* which must be acquired "first hand" from a competent fencing teacher:

a) Footwork, including the advance and retreat.
b) The lunge and recovery.
c) The foil grip and parry positions.
d) The riposte, both direct and indirect.
e) Attacks, including feints and beats.
f) "Right-of-way" and its practical application within the context of "tempo."
g) Judging and directing.
h) Practical fencing experience against an accomplished fencer to gain consciousness of what it means to fence well.

While this material is rudimentary, it serves as a sound foundation with which to approach all literature relating to fencing.

THE FENCING MASTER

In some fencing circles in the United States one may receive the impression that only the Fencing Master is properly qualified to teach fencing. This misconception has created a hesitancy on the part of some potentially fine teachers and fencers to engage in fencing instruction. While the Fencing Master serves a most important function within the fencing world, it is a serious misunderstanding to insist that one should not teach without a Master's certification. The simple fact is that one may test for certification only when extensive teaching or fencing experience has been demonstrated. The Fencing Master serves his primary function at the higher levels of competitive fencing. He can usually be found offering instruction on a professional basis in the private fencing club or coaching a varsity team for a university or college. The best of them prepare our Olympic and World Championship teams for international competition. In effect, the Fencing Master finds his primary occupation serving people who are accomplished in fencing.

If one wishes to gain Master's certification in the United States, specific requirements must be met, as set forth by the National Fencing Coaches' Association of America. The N.F.C.A.A. will authorize a committee to administer written, oral, and practical examinations to the applicant. Upon positive completion of the examinations, a Master's Certification will be issued. While the vast majority of our excellent fencing teachers and coaches are not certified as "Masters," it is they who create the broad base of fencing activity on both recreational and competitive levels in the United States. They serve as catalysts to another generation of young people and give fencing a proper place among the acknowledged lifetime sports of America.

Ideally, a fencing class is the most favorable environment in which to learn fencing. Here one may find a variety of skill levels and experience represented. The greater the competitive diversity the better, especially after the first year of training. Also, the class situation provides the teacher with an opportunity to give needed criticism which is objective and conducive to better technique and strategies as they are needed. Learning to fence is interesting, fun, and exciting, but real proficiency is gained gradually at first. The techniques of fencing are not difficult to understand, but basic technique cannot be acquired without consistent effort over a relatively extended period of time. The body and the mind need time in which to adjust to the demands of fencing. All the advanced skills in fencing depend on a sound foundation. The beginning fencer must ensure that basic material is practiced with careful attention to detail. Fencing is one of the few sports that demands the participant to have technical capabilities to play. Unlike baseball, basketball, or tennis, where one may by and large learn the game while playing, fencing requires that certain skills be reasonably mastered before one engages in play. The guard, basic footwork, parries, and attacks must be learned before one can expect reasonable success in combat. As a rule of thumb, four hours of practice per week for four weeks should provide the beginner with the necessary fundamentals with which to start sparring sessions.

SPARRING

As in boxing, it is unwise to fence with a serious competitive attitude before one has gained several hours of controlled *sparring* experience. The sparring session allows one to concentrate on self control, proper technique, and to explore different strategies. Serious competitive fencing without continuous hours of sparring practice as a background leads to poor habits in balance, technique, and strategy.

There are no shortcuts to the development of a good game. There are no natural talents in fencing. Each fencer must develop his or her own game within the framework of personal physical and mental pre-dispositions. The task is to develop an understanding of the essential nature of the fencing, and to formulate an approach that is suited to one's individual character and physical stature.

LEARNING PROCESS

To a beginner, every new technique will seem hopelessly difficult. The basic techniques of fencing are not natural and must be learned. However, with reasonable practice these same techniques will become effortless. A good part of the incentive in fencing is the discovery that the impossible techniques of yesterday are performed with ease today— a true sense of accomplishment. The situation is not unlike that of a child learning to use eating utensils. At first the task seems impossible, but eventually one is barely aware of the fork in one's hand. The fumbling efforts of the beginner are transformed into an effortless dexterity.

WINNING AND LOSING

The beginner must become accustomed to losing. There is virtually no way that a beginner can defeat an advanced fencer. The first-year fenc-er will invariably lose to the second-year fencer, just as the second-year fencer has little hope of defeating the third-year fencer. It is generally agreed that it takes about five years to develop a strong game. The beginner, unless prewarned, may find only frustration when confronted with an advanced opponent. However, this should not offer dis-couragement. Advanced fencers will always be helpful and understanding, for they remember their own fencing development as they came up through the ranks. The advanced fencer enjoys fencing the beginner. Against the beginner one may practice a new technique that may be impossible to try out against one's peers. For the beginner, this experience will show what it is the advanced fencer is trying to master. It offers a learning experience which is impossible to duplicate. The beginner can always find lively competition with his peers, wherein one may enjoy a victory now and then. Remember, all losses are forgotten with one's first victory. At this moment the hard work involved with practice becomes exhilaratingly worthwhile.

CHAPTER 3

EQUIPMENT

Good equipment is mandatory for good fencing. Proper equipment, which includes a fencing uniform, glove, mask, and foil, will ensure safety as well as comfort. When purchasing equipment, never cut costs. Excellent equipment costs little more than the lower-quality goods, and it lasts for years. Compared to that of other sports, fencing equipment is inexpensive. There is no reason to have anything but the best.

THE MASK

The fencing mask protects the eyes, ears, nose, mouth, and throat. There is little comfort in having a blade run up one's nose or into the mouth or ears. *Never* fence without this essential piece of fencing gear. The fencing mask should be lightweight and should include a reinforcement bar running down or across the front which adds strength to the wire mesh that covers the face. After fencing, the mask should be wiped clean of perspiration and stored in a dry place to prevent rust or mildew. The mask is adjustable to any head size and should offer perfect fencing vision.

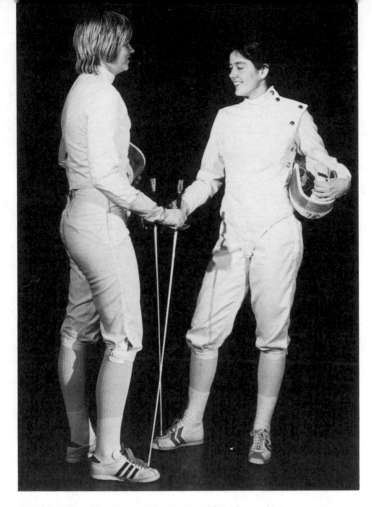

Fig. 3.1. The fencing uniform should be form-fitting, comfortable, and free of unnecessary wrinkles against which points may snag.

THE FENCING JACKET

The fencing jacket is designed to give complete protection to the torso, neck, and arms from the hardest thrusts of fencing competition. However, the primary function of the jacket is to protect one against the occasional broken blade, which is unbending and jagged-edged at the point of break. The foil jacket is made of 12-ounce duck or polyester cotton material and is double-lined for added protection on the sword-arm side of the body, which faces one's opponent and thus receives the most abuse. Jackets are made for men and women as well as for the left- or right-handed fencer.

FENCING TROUSERS

Fencing trousers may be either ankle length or knee length. The knee-length knickers are most popular and I would personally recommend them. They offer exceptional freedom in movement, especially for the stretching action of the lunge. Fencing trousers are designed without a fly to give protection to the groin area and are double-lined on the sword-arm side of the body to give complete protection to the thigh. They are made for both men and women and the left-and right-handed fencer. Knee length white socks are necessary with knickers to give protection to the ankles and shins.

GLOVE

The fencing glove protects the knuckles of the foil hand and has an extended cuff which fits *over* the sleeve of the jacket. This is designed to prevent blades from entering the jacket sleeve. (See Fig. 3.2.) The sleeve is *always* tucked into the glove, preventing injury to the arm and armpit. When selecting a glove, choose one which is slightly snug. The glove will stretch with use, creating a fit which will be nicely contoured to the hand. The foil glove should fit as perfectly as possible to prevent finger blisters and to allow a sensitive relationship between the foil handle and the hand.

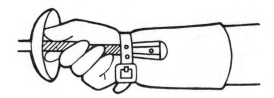

Fig. 3.2. The fencing glove with wrist strap.

WRIST STRAP

The wrist strap is used by many fencers to give added strength to the foil grip. (See Fig. 3.2.) Beginners should never use a wrist strap because it can easily become a "crutch" for the grip and prevent flexibility in foil manipulation. The fencer should resort to a wrist strap only if it is clear after extensive fencing experience that he or she does not have the strength to use the foil without one.

THE FOIL

The standard French foil is recommended to all first-year fencers. A good foil will consist of a reasonably stiff blade which bends evenly; a leather-wrapped handle, which wears longer than the cord-wrapped models; and a steel rolled-edged guard. The steel guard is recommended to the beginner in place of the lighter duraluminum guards which are available. The duraluminum guard does not hold up to the abuse the beginner is certain to inflict upon it. For more on the foil, read Chapter 4.

Foil Blades

Foil blades are available in two lengths, which are designated by the numbers 4 or 5 stamped on the blade. The number 5 blade, which is 34½ inches long, is one inch longer than the number 4 blade. The difference in length affects the balance of the weapon. While the vast majority of fencers prefer the number 5 blade, there are those who prefer the lightness of the number 4. I would recommend the number 5 blade to gain the advantage of that extra inch of reach. It is advisable to have one or two spare blades on hand. Blades break frequently, and they are relatively inexpensive.

WOMEN'S INNER PROTECTORS

The inner protector is worn under the fencing jacket. (See Fig. 3.3.) This quilted vest is designed to provide additional protection to the sensitive breast area. Breast protectors made of aluminum or wire mesh are also available to those who prefer them in place of the quilted vest.

Fig. 3.3. Women's protective vest.

Fig. 3.4. Protective sleeve.

PROTECTIVE SLEEVE

The protective sleeve gives extra protection to the sword arm and chest. It is mandatory for all N.C.A.A. and A.F.L.A. competition and is recommended for the recreational fencer as well. It is worn under the fencing jacket on the sword-arm side. (See Fig. 3.4.)

FOOTWEAR

For the beginner, any rubber-soled tennis shoe will do for fencing. An oxford style shoe is recommended for lightness, comfort, and appearance. For the serious fencer, specially designed fencing shoes are available through most sporting goods stores and fencing equipment distributors. This excellent footwear offers perfect traction and lightness and will outlast a tennis shoe several times over. For those who fence frequently or participate in tournament fencing, a fencing shoe is strongly recommended to cushion against the particular stresses and strains that fencing imposes on the feet.

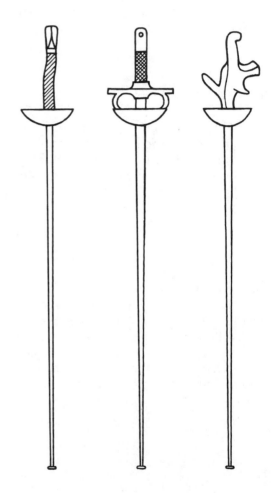

Fig. 4.1. Foils; from left to right:
French, Italian, and pistol or
orthopedic grip.

CHAPTER 4

THE FOIL AND RULES OF PLAY

THE FOIL

While the foil is best thought of as a "tool" to facilitate efficient offensive and defensive action, it offers another potential relating to tactical analysis. Used properly, the foil becomes a sensitive instrument with which one may probe, explore, and intimidate an opponent's intentions. One must be aware that the foil is the focal point of fencing attention. All movements of the blade, including blade contact, will assuredly deliver strong impressions to the opponent, leading him or her into traps and confused concentration. Successful fencing demands that one utilize the full potential of the "foil language." Failure to do so will severely limit the fencer's ability to discover the uncontrolled reflex responses of the opponent, and it is these responses which will form the basis of the fencer's offensive strategy. The fencer who is not aware of the foil's potential will assuredly be victimized by it.

Of the three basic types of foils, the French and Italian are traditional, while the orthopedic grip has made its appearance only within the last thirty years. (See Fig. 4.1.) the Italian foil is seen less frequently because it is not well suited to the modern electric foil game, where thrusts to traditionally obscure areas of the target have become commonplace. In the face of change, the French foil holds its own with remarkable success, proving its versatility in all fencing styles. The orthopedic grip has proven effective primarily in the context of electrical fencing, and a large variety of orthopedic designs are now available and in use throughout the world.

The past twenty years have witnessed a strong trend toward the use of the orthopedic grip on all levels of fencing. However, while many feel the orthopedic, or "pistol grip," offers many advantages in strength and speed, it is generally recognized that the French handle is most suited for first-year instruction. The beginning fencer must develop *control* as his or her first objective in training. Without the ability to place the point on target, speed, power, and sound tactical judgment are only interesting speculations. The French handle, by virtue of its simplicity, creates the best advantage for the development of sensitivity and controlled power.

The French Foil

The French foil is composed of five distinct parts: the pommel, handle, thumb pad, bell guard, and blade. It is important to know the function of each of these components. The foil is the fencer's only mechanical means to accomplishment, and a familiarity with its makeup leads to better performance. (See Fig. 4.2.)

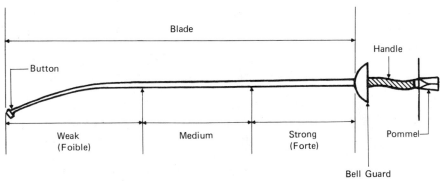

Fig. 4.2. The French foil.

The pommel. The pommel holds the foil together and balances the blade. A heavy pommel will act as a counterbalance to the blade, giving it a sense of lightness to the tip. A lightweight pommel will have the opposite effect, giving the blade a feeling of weight. The standard French pommel is best, at least until one has fenced enough to develop a preference for a particular balance. If the blade is broken, one need only unscrew the pommel, replace the broken blade and secure the pommel back in place.

The handle. The foil handle is designed to allow maximum finger control for the manipulation of the blade, as well as to create a grip which conveniently lends itself to the thrusting and defensive movements of fencing. The curve in the handle is designed to fit the contour of the large muscle at the base of the thumb. A variety of French handles are available for different-sized hands and for right- and left-handed fencers.

The thumb pad. A thumb pad is placed inside the guard to give a cushioned protection to the knuckles of the sword hand. In the event of a collision between the foil guards of two attacking fencers, the thumb pad may well save one the pain of bruised or broken fingers. *Never* fence without this simple but essential piece of equipment.

The bell guard. The bell guard protects the hand from slashing actions which are unavoidably a part of fencing. However, the guard's prime function is to aid in the execution of parries. Most parries depend on the guard for control of the adversary's blade during defense. Maximum size for the guard is four inches in diameter, while guards as small as three inches are available. The standard four-inch guard is most popular and is recommended. There are many models of guards, ranging from the strong steel rolled-edged to the relatively fragile duraluminum designs, which are preferred in competition because of their lightness.

The blade. The part of the blade upon which the guard, handle, and pommel are attached is called the "tang." The tip of the blade, which is flattened for safety, is called the "button." The length of the blade from the button to the guard is divided into three parts for tactical convenience. The first third of the blade nearest the guard is the "strong." The middle section is the "medium," and the third nearest the button is the "weak." Each of these three areas serves a specific purpose to the fencer.

The *strong* of the blade is used exclusively for *defense.* It is through the combined relationship of the *strong* and the guard that most parries are created. The *medium* of the blade is used primarily for *actions against the opponent's blade* in preparation for attacks. Beats, presses, and binds are all performed using the offensive advantages of the medium. The medium may also be used for the specialized spanking parries used frequently by advanced fencers.

The *weak* of the blade is used for reconnaissance movements such as beats, taps, and pressures against the adversary's blade. These are designed to draw or sound out involuntary information from one's opponent relating to nervous habits and reflex responses which can be used against him or her. In effect, the weak of the blade allows one a means to explore the mental state of one's adversary.

Note that the blade is not straight, but rather is bent slightly downward from the medium forward. The bend functions to give maximum opportunity for a secure touch. In effect, the blade hooks into the target, giving a better opportunity for a touch that will not slip off or pass by.

The foil is a carefully designed offensive and defensive weapon. Its potential is virtually unlimited to the fencer who uses it to best advantage.

THE GRIP

A correct grip is essential to fencing. The French handle is held in a manner that permits the fingers and forearm to control the movements of the foil. When learning to hold the foil, the grip will at first seem weak, awkward, and contrived. A few hours of practice, paying careful attention to the properties of the grip, will be needed before one can feel comfortable and at home with the foil.

Technique of the Grip

The thumb is placed flat on top of the handle directly above the index finger. The bottom of the handle opposite the thumb must rest securely on top of the *first joint* of the index finger. (See Fig. 4.3.) Two of the remaining fingers are placed on the *side* of the handle, so that *only the finger pads* are in contact with the handle. *The fingers must not be allowed to curl over and around the handle.* With the fingers positioned correctly, the grip should be held lightly, allowing a space between the palm and the handle. (See Fig. 4.4.) Under no circumstances must the palm be permitted to press against the handle, causing rigidity and tension in the hand. When holding the foil correctly, one should be able to easily insert the index finger of the other hand between the palm and the handle. (See Fig. 4.5.) This "finger test" is a handy reminder to the beginner, who, when feeling the initial insecurity of the grip, will invariably adjust the handle to fit tightly into his or her palm, causing the

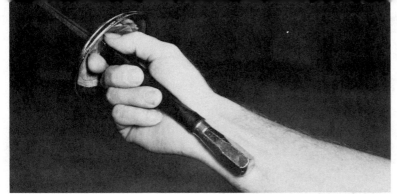

Fig. 4.3. The thumb and index fingers rest above and below each other. These fingers are traditionally referred to as manipulators, since they control the movements of the foil blade.

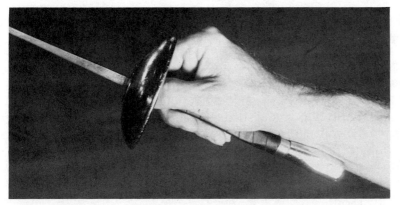

Fig. 4.4. The hand is relaxed with the pommel resting gently against the wrist. A traditional analogy suggests that the foil be held like a bird, strongly enough to keep it in hand, but not strongly enough to cause injury.

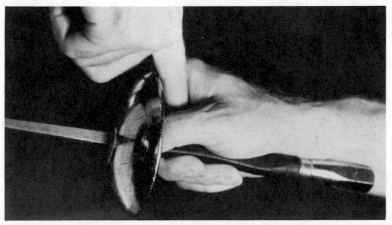

Fig. 4.5. This finger test is an excellent reminder to the beginner who is inclined to choke the foil during the initial weeks of training.

fingers to curl up and around the handle. Don't choke the foil! If the fingers cramp and ache during practice, it simply means the foil is being held too tight.

Held correctly, *the blade becomes an extension of the forearm*; one can visualize a line from the elbow to the tip of the foil, which should rest at a level even with the shoulders. (See Fig. 7.2.) It is a common error to hold the foil too high, placing the point well above the head.

PRACTICE

The foil and accompanying technique are best concentrated on for practice after one has learned the guard position and basic footwork, which includes the advance and retreat. Once a sense of physical stance and footwork is established, the student will absorb technique relating to the foil more easily.

During the more advanced stages of practice and competition, the fencer may want to graduate to the orthopedic grip. "A fencer is well advised to change to the revolver (pistol) grip when he has already learned to master technique perfectly with the French grip and has made absolutely sure that it does not suit him at all."* It is my opinion that a fencer has no business with the orthopedic grip during the first three years of his or her development.

COURTESY

The salute before a fencing bout and the handshake after are the only pure rituals of the modern game. The importance of this ritual or formality cannot be overstated when one considers the psychological implications of fencing. While fencing is, perhaps, the most sophisticated encounter to be found in competitive sports, it nevertheless is a fight in which an enormous amount of nervous energy is expended. Tempers are easily lost in the heat of competition. The fencer who suffers defeat cannot escape the momentary feeling that he or she has been beaten on all psychic levels. A fencer's intellectual and physical self-image has been put through a difficult test. The salute and handshake serve to remind the contestants that, after all, this is only a game

---

*Lukovich, Istvan: *Electric Foil Fencing.* Corvina Press, 1971, p. 33.

Fig. 4.6. The salute.

in which they are voluntary participants, with full knowledge that they cannot win all of the time.

The Salute

Before the fencing bout begins, whether it be unsupervised recreation or serious competition, the principals salute each other. The salute should avoid dramatic flourishes and be done in a friendly manner after genuine eye contact has been made. The salute should consist only of a crisp dip of the foil blade in the direction of one's opponent. This acknowledges the understanding that every effort will be made to win the bout according to the rules and conventions of fair play, and that, regardless of feelings when the bout is over, a genuine handshake will be offered in appreciation of the learning experience and enjoyment that each fencer has received.

Fig. 4.7. The conclusion of a hard-fought fencing bout.

Shaking Hands

The handshake must be sincere, especially if one has lost the contest. This act of touching dismisses strong feelings, bringing the fencer back to normal social focus, where animosities, possibly engendered during competition, may be left on the "fencing ground."

The fencing world recognizes the need of a competition where the individual can "let it all come out." The salute and handshake are the essential courtesies that define the beginning and the end of an occasion in which this release can take place in a constructive, civilized, and exciting manner.

THE READY POSITION

Preparing for Guard

The beginning student needs an orientation point from which he or she may step forward into the guard position. It is advisable to give careful consideration to this initial stance, or "ready position," which must be assumed before saluting one's adversary or stepping into the guard at the beginning of a fencing bout. (See Fig. 4.8.) The ready position allows the fencers a brief moment to feel the correctness of their bodies and to focus their attention. In effect, the fencer uses the ready position

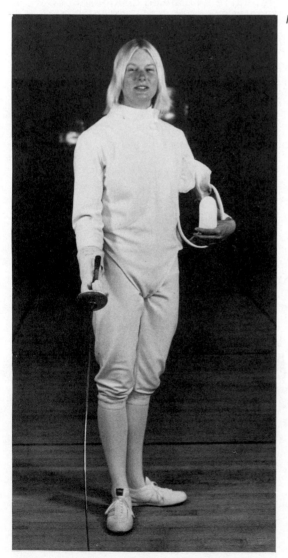

Fig. 4.8. The ready position.

to "get the head in order" for the kind of concentration which will be needed after the command to "fence" is given. From the ready position one should always step *forward* into the guard. This habit will aid in the perfection of the guard position. A forward step to the guard is natural, and economical in movement and can easily be coordinated. Stepping backward creates an ungainly and uncoordinated movement. Also, stepping forward shows the opponent that one is confidently ready and willing to fence. A backward step reveals timidity, which always gives one's adversay a psychological boost; this can easily cost one the winning point in a difficult bout.

All movements in fencing require a balanced relationship between head and torso, a right angle position of the feet, and total relaxation. This stance contributes to better physical movement and lucid awareness of the bouting situation. If these considerations are present in the ready position, the fencer has an excellent chance to bring them forward into the guard and ultimately into every initiated action of the bout.

Common Errors

The two most common errors of the ready position are:

a) Failure to assume the position through ignorance of its importance and function.
b) Placing too much emphasis on stance, which creates tension and stiffness in the body, similiar to the attention position of a military drill.

SCORING AND RULES OF PLAY

The Touch

To be valid, the "touch" in foil fencing must score on the target areas, which include the front, sides, and back of the torso. (See Fig. 4.9.) All touches that score to the head, arms, and legs of the body are considered "foul" or "off-target" hits. In standard nonelectric foil the touch is scored by reaching the target area with the point of the weapon with sufficient strength to bend the blade visibly. With electric foil the "button" on the tip of the blade must be depressed, completing an electrical circuit which registers the touch on the scoring machine. In both instances, the touch must arrive with enough penetrating power to inflict a *theoretical* wound.

Fig. 4.9. Touches must land on the target areas, shown here in black, to be valid scoring points.

Right-of-way

The rules governing the *method* of foil fencing apply equally to standard or electric technique through the concept of *right-of-way*. This concept states that every valid attack must be defended against as though one's life were actually being threatened. The defender who ignores the attack does so at his or her own risk. The right-of-way attempts to preserve the reality of the dueling ground, where at all costs the objective is to deliver fatal hits without losing one's life in the process. The fencer is allowed to dodge, sidestep, retreat, or parry as a form of defense. However, in the event both fencers are simultaneously scored against, creating the "double touch," the fencer who possesses the right-of-way is awarded the point. The winner's final movement leading to the double hit is determined theoretically in keeping with the law of self-preservation. The opponent who has lost has made a move which, on the dueling ground, would have been suicidal. In short, the right-of-way ensures that the fencer will compete as though he or she were a rational human being faced with a sharp and lethal weapon.

Right-of-way is the *logic of fencing strategy*. Where balance is the key to effective movement, right-of-way is its counterpart in strategy. If an understanding of right-of-way is developed early, the fencer can progress more rapidly. If the fencer knows why a poorly-executed attack or parry loses right-of-way, he or she will instinctively develop a sensitive, fast, and controlled game. Most of all, the beginner must learn that all technique and conditioning in modern fencing is designed for one end, to capture the right-of-way.

Many of our young fencers do not understand this premise. Often, fencers labor under the misconception that instruction relating to right-of-way should be reserved until one has gained competence in the techniques of the bouting situation. The fencer who does not understand the rules will usually contrive his or her own, which invariably work against overall progress. As in physical conditioning, poor habits in strategy are difficult to correct once they take root.

The following are the rules of right-of-way as they appear in the A.F.L.A. rules book.

1. *The fencer attacked is alone counted as touched—*
   a) if he makes a stop into a simple attack;
   b) if, instead of parrying, he attempts to avoid being touched and fails;
   c) if, after a successful parry, he pauses for a moment—which gives his opponent the right to resume his attack (redoublement, remise, or reprise);
   d) if, on the composite attack, he makes a stop without having the advantage of a period of fencing time;
   e) if, being in line (arm extended and point threatening a valid surface) after a beat or a taking of the blade which deflects his weapon, he attacks or replaces his blade in line instead of parrying a direct thrust made by the attacker.

2. *The attacker alone is counted as touched—*
   a) if he starts his attack when the opponent is in line (arm extended and point threatening a valid surface) without deflecting the opposing blade;
   b) if he attempts to find the blade and fails (because of a derobement or troumpment) and still continues the attack;
   c) if, in a composite attack, in the course of which his opponent finds the blade, he continues the attack while his opponent immediately ripostes;
   d) if, in a composite attack, he is hit by a stop made with the advantage of a period of fencing time before his conclusion;
   e) if he touches by remise, redoublement, or reprise, after a parry by his opponent which is followed by an immediate simple riposte executed in one period of fencing.

3. *The fencer is replaced on guard* every time that the director cannot decide clearly which side is at fault in a double hit.

After the fencer has gained a basic orientation to right-of-way (parry when attacked, riposte after parrying, and don't attack into attacks), a good portion of practice should be involved with experience directing and judging bouts. Informal round-robin tournaments, where the fencer has an opportunity to direct and judge, are excellent. This type of experience teaches the importance of right-of-way better than any other method. However, an instructor or experienced fencer should be available to make corrections when the inevitable mistakes are made.

BOUTING

All competitive fencing is performed through the conventions of the bouting situation. When one of the contestants has been scored *against* five times, he or she is declared the loser and the bout is terminated. It is important to note that all scores are counted against rather than for the fencer. A perfect winning score is "0", while a defeat is always 5 points. The score may be 5–0, 5–1, 5–2, 5–3, or 5–4 but never 5–5. There are no tied bout scores in fencing. After each *valid* touch is scored, the fencers return to the "guard line,"* where fencing is resumed for the next touch. The bout is terminated when one of the contestants has accumulated five touches against him or herself or when the designated fencing time has run out. All bouts are fenced for five touches or six minutes of fencing time. When time runs out, the scores of each fencer are advanced until one of them reaches a terminating score. For example, if time runs out while the score is 4–1, a point is added to each score, resulting in a 5–2 loss for one of the fencers. If the bout score is tied at the conclusion of fencing time, the fencers are allowed to fence until a deciding touch has been scored. The director of the bout must officially warn each fencer when one minute of fencing time remains.

---

*See Chapter 11, "Judging and Directing Standard Foil."

Fig. 5.1. The guard position.

CHAPTER 5

THE GUARD POSITION

PURPOSE OF THE GUARD

The guard position is not to be considered a strictly defensive position as its name implies. Rather, the guard is better viewed as a neutral stance from which the fencer may attack or defend, depending on circumstances. It is from the guard position that the fencer observes the adversary for unconscious flaws in technique that tell one when to defend, attack, or get out of distance. The guard offers the only time during the bout when the fencer has the opportunity for analysis and formulation of tactics.

From a mechanical point of view the stance of the guard should give the fencer a capability to defend or attack effortlessly at a split second notice. The guard must be perfectly balanced, favoring neither defense nor offense. It must always be ready to receive or deliver the unexpected. (See Fig. 5.1.)

MECHANICS OF THE GUARD

For instructional purposes, the guard can be broken down into five parts, each of which performs a specific function. It is important that the student understand each part and its relationship to its counterparts. This information enables the fencers to trace their own mistakes and to make their own corrections when inevitable errors occur.

1.   Feet Position

The feet form a right angle approximately one-and-a-half of the fencer's own foot lengths apart. The tall fencer may add two or three inches to this stance. The right foot must point directly at one's adversary, which serves as a "gunsight" for the attack.* (See Figs. 5.2, 5.3, 5.4.)

---

*For ease of reading, all descriptive material is addressed to the right-handed fencer. Left-handers should reverse directions.

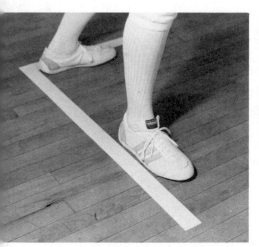
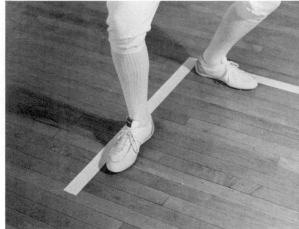

Figures 5.2, 5.3, 5.4

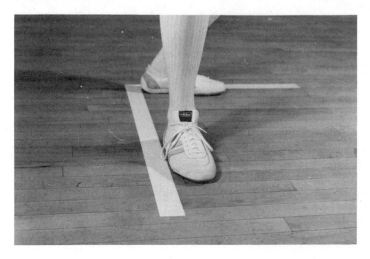

2. Knee Position

The legs should be positioned so that by placing the left knee directly over the left toes and the right knee directly behind the right toes, the weight of the body will be equally distributed on both legs. The knees must not be allowed to turn in toward each other. This will weaken the stance and diminish power for the lunge. It is impossible to develop a strong lunge without sufficient bend in the knees. It is acknowledged that the knee position, which sets the stage for the lunge, is one of the most physically demanding of fencing postures for the beginner. Leg power in fencing is essential, and the student must practice until strength is developed which will transform the knee position into an effortless stance.

3. Left Arm Position

The left arm is held high in preparation for the attack. A forceful downward action of the left arm helps give forward momentum to the lunge. The lunge receives its power from the combined push of the left leg and the sharp downward motion of the left arm.

4. Sword Arm Position

The sword arm is held in a neutral position between the high and low lines of the target area, allowing equal defensive capability for the upper and lower torso. The shoulder should be relaxed, and the elbow should be approximately the distance of a hand-spread from the hip. The hand is held in sixte position (to be discussed in Chapter 6), inviting all opposing offensive action to the inside line.

It is most important that the fencer maintain sixte position as a neutral "home base" for his or her defensive orientation. If the hand drifts into a central guard position, the sixte line will open, creating two vulnerable lines to defend.* This common error gives one's opponent too many possibilities for scoring. One line is difficult to defend, two lines are impossible.

5. Torso Position

The torso position should give a three-quarter view of the fencer to the opponent. If the torso position is correct, the other parts of the guard position will fall into place quite naturally with just a small amount of practice. Many fencers show a complete profile to their opponents, thinking that the smaller target exposed as a result will create some

---

*See Chapter 7, "Defense and Parry Systems."

advantage. While this may be true for exceptionally thin, loose-jointed people, it will work only to the disadvantage of the vast majority of fencers. Profiling in the guard position places strain on the shoulders, neck, and right thigh, making it difficult to maintain the guard in sixte and impossible to keep the knees apart.

Finally, the head should rest comfortably on top of the spine and should be turned so the eyes rest directly on one's opponent.

PRACTICE

It is advisable to learn the parts of the guard position in separate consecutive order. After this material has been digested, the fencer should do drill stepping from the "ready position" forward into the "on guard" stance. This practice should be carried out until one can step into guard perfectly. For the beginner, practicing in front of a mirror is a convenient way to check one's progress.

It is important to spend the extra time to review this basic material. Faulty habits of the guard such as crooked feet, straight legs, poor balance, and tension will carry over to affect the footwork and lunge. The guard is the fencer's foundation and it must be correct if it is to be strong.

Common Errors

Tension and loss of balance are the beginner's most common errors. The more extroverted personalities will be inclined to favor the right leg, while the introverts will favor the left leg. Many students try too hard and must consciously try to relax. The fencer must keep in mind that the guard position will feel awkward at first, but after a few weeks, will feel perfectly natural. There is no rush, and in the meantime there are other things to learn.

CHAPTER 6

BASIC FOOTWORK

IMPORTANCE OF FOOTWORK

Footwork is the key to mobility and is indispensable to good fencing. Through footwork the fencer becomes a master at maintaining control of distance, never allowing the opponent knowledge of how far one must travel to score. Footwork accomplishes this by creating freedom of movement forward or backward at any given moment of the fencing bout.

The Advance

The advance is made by first stepping forward with the right foot, which touches the floor *heel first* and is immediately followed by the forward step of the left foot. The completion of the step of the right foot, as the ball of the foot moves downward to the floor, should be exactly coordinated with the left foot's forward motion, allowing *both feet to settle on the floor simultaneously*. It is a common error to complete the step of the right foot before the left foot makes its move. As the advance is made, the fencer must ensure that the knees stay bent and the right-angle positioning of the feet is maintained. The feet should not slide or drag on the floor.

The advance serves the purpose of moving the fencer forward to gain a possible opportunity for the attack, or to draw the opponent's attack into a prepared and waiting defense. In either case the advance should always be performed with utmost caution and awareness that it will offer a split-second opportunity in which to attack or defend. It becomes evident that the guard, balance, and mental alertness must not be lost during this most crucial moment of the fencing bout.

The Retreat

The retreat is performed by stepping backward with the left foot, which is followed immediately by the backward step of the right foot. At the completion of the retreat the feet should retain their original right-angle position and, as in the advance, they should not slide or drag.

The normal reaction to an opponent who has proven that he or she can deliver a devastating offensive is to retreat. The retreat should be practiced as a long step backward, for it is most frequently executed as an escape from attack. It is impossible in today's game to defend successfully without the retreat. The speed of modern fencing requires that the retreat be integrated as part of the parry system for defensive protection. The fencers who stand their ground during defense should not be surprised to discover their opponent's blade bending securely on their chest.

Practice

Footwork lends itself beautifully to drill and warm-up sessions. Every practice session should include a minimum of ten minutes for footwork exercises. The advance and retreat must be practiced in multiple combinations, for example: advance, retreat; double advance, double retreat; double retreat, advance; advance, triple retreat. The combinations are endless. Advancing rapidly the length of a gymnasium and retreating back again is excellent conditioning. The fencer should practice all footwork without loss of balance or the guard position. All footwork must be light and relaxed. Relaxation is always more important than mechanical perfection, but if one can have both, all the better.

CHAPTER 7

DEFENSE AND PARRY SYSTEMS

TRADITIONAL LINES OF DEFENSE

When in the guard position, the fencer's foil blade should define the four "lines of defense" in the target area. For example, when the foil is held in the *traditional guard* of "central position," it will create four specific areas of the target which must be protected from attack. (See Fig. 7.l.) The exposed target area above the foil blade is the "high line," while the target area exposed below the blade is the "low line." The target area to the right of the blade is the "outside line," and the target area to the blade's left is the "inside line." The problem of defense becomes immediately complex, for the best defensive movements can expect to protect only one "line" at any given moment of "fencing time" or "tempo,"* leaving three lines unprotected. This allows the attacker three undefended lines in which to score at any given moment of the fencing bout. All defensive strategy is performed with this consideration foremost in mind. The fencer must be sure that the line he or she defends is the line in which the attacker attempts to score.

---

*"Fencing time (or period of fencing time; 'temps d'escrime') is the time required to perform one simple fencing action."

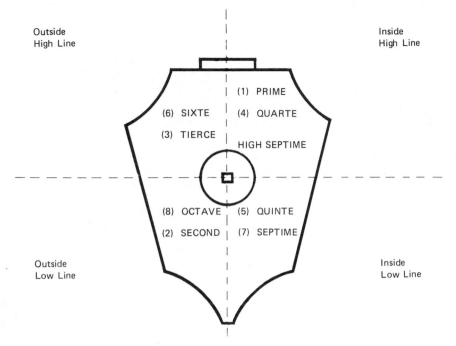

Fig. 7.1. Foil guard in central position.

Fig. 7.2. Foil guard in sixte position.

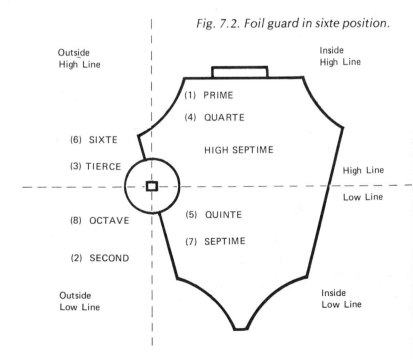

Fig. 7.3. The guard parry of sixte.

THE MODERN GUARD IN SIXTE

The *sixte guard* has replaced the traditional central guard position. (See Fig. 7.2.) The reason for this change becomes clear when these two methods of defense are compared. It has been observed that the traditional central guard creates four lines of vulnerability. The modern fencer has discovered pragmatically that by shifting the guard from central position to the sixte position one eliminates the two outside defense lines, leaving only the high and low inside lines open to immediate attack.

Observe that the sixte guard places the entire target area on the inside line. This is far-reaching in its implications. By shifting the guard to sixte the fencer knows that all attacks that initially address themselves to the outside line are harmless and can be ignored. In contrast, observe that the traditional guard in central position exposes both the outside line and the inside line to attack. Consequently, the guard in sixte has an astonishing superiority over the traditional central guard, which never knows for certain which line will be attacked. The modern fencer cannot afford the tactical insecurity of central guard position and so must always maintain a sixte guard.

A second consideration favoring the sixte guard concerns the relative strengths of the parries which protect the opposing inside and outside lines. It must be observed that the parries protecting the inside lines are the strongest because pressure from the attack is forced into and against the palm of the hand, whereas parries to the outside line receive pressure away from the palm and against the fingers, which weakens the grip. It is always to the defender's advantage to receive attacks with his or her strongest parries. Fencing in the sixte guard position is the best way to ensure this situation. A third consideration which favors a guard in sixte is the relative naturalness and ease with which the quarte parry is made, as contrasted with the difficulty of moving from quarte to the sixte parry. It is both psychologically and physically easier to parry quarte than sixte. A quarte response is instinctive, while the sixte response is learned. It is only practical to favor the sixte position by maintaining it as one's guard, thus giving primary defensive consideration to the weakest of defensive lines.

THE PARRY

The parry can be defined as a defensive move with the foil which successfully deflects an attacking blade from the target area, preventing a valid touch. There are two major parry classifications; the first is the *guard parries*, which best uses the relationship between the strong of the blade and the foil guard as a means of defense, and second, the *spanking parries*, which are executed by implementation of a sharp, strong beat with the medium of the defending blade against the medium of the attacking blade.

TYPES OF PARRIES

The following list describes six different kinds of parries which can be recognized in modern fencing:

1. The Guard Parry

A parry which deflects the attacking blade by moving it aside with use of the guard. (See Fig. 7.4.) While this parry is used against all forms of attack, it is most effective at close defending distance. The parries of quarte, sixte, second, and octave are most suited to the guard parry defense.

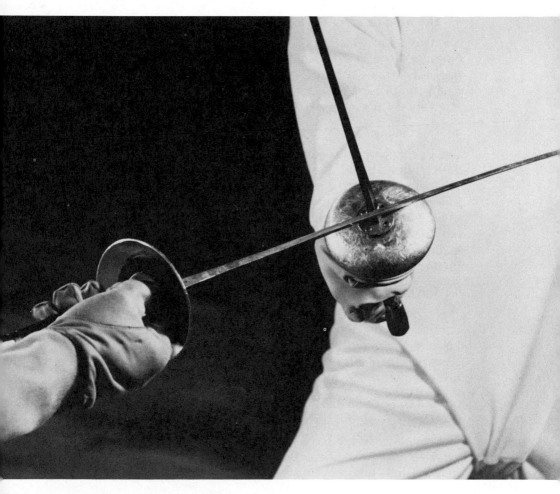

Fig. 7.4. The guard parry of quarte.

2. The Spanking Parry

A parry which deflects the attacking blade with a sharp beat delivered
to the medium of the blade. The spanking parry is specially designed to
be used as an early defense, catching the opponent's blade by surprise
before close attacking distance is established. The spanking defense is
specially suited for the parries of quarte and septime.

3. The Holding Parry

A guard parry which, after deflecting the attacking blade from line, continues to hold it in an out-of-line position. The holding parry is used primarily against opponents who remise* and are difficult to score against with a riposte,† or who can be best scored against in their recovery by use of a delayed riposte.

4. The Ceding Parry

The ceding parry is used against attacks which prepare with a binding action on the blade. The defender allows the bind to take place, maintaining a controlled pressure which gives in or cedes to the forward binding action of the offensive movement and ends in a parry position. Ceding parries are used to excellent advantage against opponents who habitually bind or wrestle on the blade during their offensive. The ceding parry is especially useful against beginners, who are prone to binding offensive attacks.

5. The Flying Parry

The flying parry is executed with a backward spanking action which continues in one motion back, over, and around‡ the tip of the attacking blade to score with a riposte to an alternate line from which the parry was made. The flying parry must be performed as one extremely fast, uninterrupted motion.

6. The Opposition Parry

A parry which performs the combined functions of deflecting the attacking blade and of scoring against the attacker's forward moving target area. In effect, the opposition parry combines the parry and the riposte§ into one movement. (See Fig. 7.5.)

TRADITIONAL PARRIES

Originally the defense system included eight parries for the protection of the four lines of the target. The parries of prime (one), second (two), tierce (three), quarte (four), quinte (five), sixte (six), septime (seven),

---

*An immediate replacement of the point at the conclusion of an attack which fails.
†A counterattack executed immediately on the conclusion of a parry. (See Chapter 9.)
‡Coupé. (See Chapter 8.)
§For ripostes see Chapter 9.

Fig. 7.5. The opposition parry from sixte.

and octave (eight) comprise the total system. Each line of the target was defended by two corresponding parries. (See Fig. 7.1.) As can be seen, the high outside line was protected by the sixte and tierce parries, while the high inside line was protected by the parries of quarte and prime. The low outside line employed the parries of second and octave, leaving septime and quinte for the defense of the low inside line.

Fig. 7.6. Prime (first) parry.   Fig. 7.7. Second parry.

MODERN DEFENSE

Because of the faster pace of modern fencing, it is impractical to base one's game on the use of all eight traditional parries. Today's advanced fencer may have knowledge of all eight of the traditional parries but will seldom, if ever, use more than four of them in a complete game. Every teacher of fencing will prefer some parries over others, emphasizing those which are thought to be of most value and consistent with a particular method of fencing. For example, it is universally agreed that the sixte parry is sufficient for total defense of the high outside line, relegating the tierce parry to an importance of historic interest only. Also, the

Fig. 7.8.
Tierce (third) parry.

Fig. 7.9.
Quarte (fourth) parry.

Fig. 7.10.
Quinte (fifth) parry.

quarte parry has become the universal defense for the high inside line, leaving the prime parry as a secondary defense, used only for special occasions on the more advanced fencing levels. There is little agreement on which parry is best suited for the low outside line; many teachers get excellent results through the use of second position while others, myself included, do just as well emphasizing octave. Quinte parry is rarely taught at all and is thought of by fencers as a low quarte innovation which is done naturally by anyone possessing a quarte defense.

Fig. 7.11.
Sixte (sixth) parry.

Fig. 7.12.
Septime (seventh) parry.

Fig. 7.13.
Octave (eighth) parry.

MODERN PARRIES

The beginner should practice only parries that are of basic practical value and which lead to sound fencing habits. The parries of sixte, quarte, octave, or second,* and septime have proven to be totally adequate for most levels of fencing and should form the basis for all beginners training in defense.

All effective parry systems ensure that in the event a given parry fails to find the attacking blade, the hand will move to the next most

---

*Octave and second are interchangeable.

probable line of vulnerability. A good parry system will couple parries together which work "back-to-back," giving protection to all areas of the target with a minimum waste of hand movement. For example, when quarte and sixte parries are executed in rapid succession, protecting the high inside and outside lines, their movement can be described as a horizontal or lateral parry system; or when sixte parry is coordinated with octave parry to protect the high and low outside lines in consecutive order, they create a vertical parry system. It is through the use of parry systems that the fencer develops a powerful defensive game.

COMBINATION PARRIES

A series of parries which are designed to protect several lines of the target area in consecutive order, and which work in combination with each other, create a parry system. The following parry systems are basic to fencing:

1. Horizontal Parry Systems

The horizontal systems will employ either sixte and quarte for protection of the high line, or octave and septime to protect the low line. (See Figs. 7.14 through 7.17.)

Figs. 7.14 and 7.15.
Sixte-quarte combination.

Figs. 7.16 and 7.17.
Octave-septime combination.

Figs. 7.18 and 7.19.
Sixte-octave combination.

Figs. 7.20 and 7.21.
Quarte-septime combination.

2. Vertical Parry Systems

The vertical systems combine either sixte and octave for protection of the outside high and low lines, or quarte and septime to protect the inside high and low lines. It should be noted that the vertical defense describes a semicircular line which gives greater protection to the target. (See Figs. 7.18 through 7.21.)

3. Diagonal Parry Systems

The diagonal system uses octave and quarte to give consecutive defense to the outside low and inside high lines. Sixte and septime work together for protection of the high outside and low inside lines. (See Figs. 7.22 through 7.25.)

Figs. 7.22 and 7.23. Octave-quarte combination.

Figs. 7.24 and 7.25. Sixte-septime combination.

4. Circular Parry Systems

The circular parry protects a given line when the foil is used to describe a defensive circular movement in its attempt to find the attacking blade. For example, if the fencer is defending the high line, the foil is moved defensively from sixte position in a counter-clockwise circular direction until it returns to sixte position. This is called a circular sixte parry. (See Fig. 7.26.) If the circular defense starts from quarte position, describing a clockwise pattern covering the target, the defender has performed a circular quarte parry. (See Fig. 7.27.) Circular octave describes a clockwise movement which defends the lower target. (See Fig. 7.28.) "Think of your grip as a tiny motor that could spin your blade

Fig. 7.26. Circular sixte parry.

Fig. 7.27. Circular quarte parry.

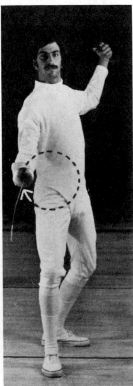
Fig. 7.28. Circular octave parry.

as fast as an airplane propeller. If the radius of the circle traced by your point would screen your whole target, no incoming steel could possibly pierce your defense. This should give you some idea."*

Figs. 7.29 and 7.30. Septime-high septime combination.

5. High Septime Parry

By raising the septime parry to a high-line position one creates a high septime parry.† We may add septime-high as a part of the system of combination parries. (See Figs. 7.29 and 7.30.)

---

*Aldo Nadi, *On Fencing*. New York: G.P. Putnam's Sons, 1943, p. 77.
†Some fencing teachers prefer to designate the high septime parry as "quinte."

COMBINED PARRY SYSTEMS

The cornerstone of defense rests in the combination of parry systems. By combining systems, the fencer can virtually build a wall of steel between himself and the adversary. Attacks which are designed to penetrate a horizontal defense can easily be stopped by using circular parries. Conversely, a horizontal defense will stop attacks which anticipate a circular parry. The fencer must never allow the opponent knowledge of which system he or she will use.

The following are a few examples of combined systems: circular sixte-quarte; circular sixte-octave; circular quarte-sixte; quarte-circular quarte-sixte; octave-quarte-sixte; octave-sixte-circular sixte-quarte.

Practice

Parries are best practiced after one has demonstrated a reasonable command of the guard in sixte in coordination with sound footwork and the ability to perform a direct attack with a smooth delivery and recovery back to the sixte guard.

The high line parries of quarte and sixte are learned first. (See Figs. 7.31 and 7.32.) Students should practice the parry positions in coordination with their footwork before practicing parries which defend against thrusts to their target. Drills where emphasis is placed on coordinated hand and foot movement are excellent. For example: retreat in quarte, retreat sixte; advance quarte, retreat sixte; advance, lunge, recover to quarte, retreat sixte; lunge, parry quarte, recover to sixte, retreat quarte, retreat sixte, etc. This is not unlike shadow boxing. During drill practice one must remember that all parries must be executed properly and with a minimum of effort. The hands should move smoothly while the blade gives full protection to each line corresponding to a given parry position. The physical stance of the guard should be relaxed, intact, and on balance throughout the drill.

Practicing parry combinations develops excellent blade control. It is beneficial to practice in front of a mirror to gain a better perspective of how the combinations relate to each other.

PARTNERSHIP TRAINING

When the student begins to feel at home with the demands of the drill, it is advisable to start practicing with a partner. It is best to practice

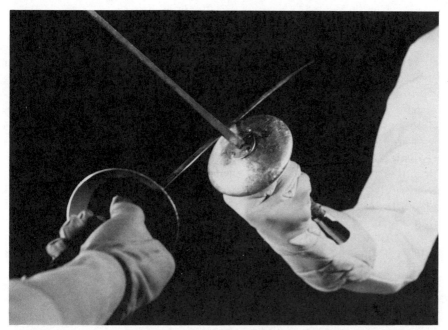

Fig. 7.31. Sixte parry. Note that when parrying sixte the foil hand is turned slightly over to the outside line. Also, the foil tip does not drop, remaining high.

Fig. 7.32. Quarte parry. When parrying quarte the foil is rolled slightly to the inside line with the top of the foil remaining high.

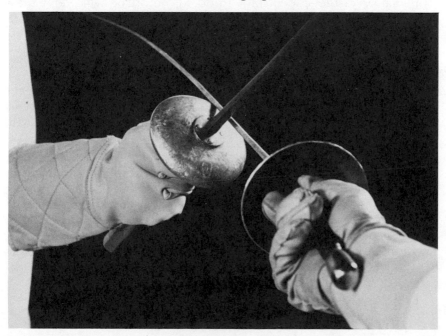

direct attacks against appropriate parries with each other. Each fencer should alternate his or her offensive and defensive role thus learning what a parry feels like against an oncoming attack, as well as experiencing having an attack parried, with the resultant problem of recovery. Practice must emphasize the importance of clean, well-executed thrusts that are delivered strictly to the high line, which allows the defender a realistic opportunity to practice specific parries. It is impossible to practice the quarte or sixte parries if one's partner insists upon delivering the practice attacks to the low line areas. It is each fencer's responsibility to see that his or her partner cooperates to ensure sound practice habits.

Partnership practice must initially be done *slowly*, giving priority to precise execution. As the student becomes more accomplished, the pace of practice can be increased, placing emphasis on speed as well as control. Partnership training will develop self-control, which in the final analysis is one of the fencer's prime assets. It is advisable to exchange partners frequently to gain experience through a variety of responses. No two fencers react in the same manner.

Common Errors

During the first session of partnership practice one may observe errors which are common to all beginning students and should be corrected immediately. If the student fails to do so, he or she will adopt these errors as fencing habits which are nearly impossible to correct once they have been established.

1. When parrying, the beginners, as a reflex reaction to the attack, will suck in their stomachs, withdrawing backwards while straightening their legs. One must be constantly reminded that the torso should remain erect with the knees bent during all defensive response. One must practice letting the hand do the parrying without accompanying physical contortions.

2. When parrying, beginners will stiffen their arms forward in an attempt to push the oncoming blade away from their bodies; this invariably causes the point of the foil to drop out of parry position, losing control of the incoming blade and causing it to score somewhere in the area of the legs and groin. The beginner must be reminded that during all high-line parries it is imperative that the *arm stay back* and the *point remain high*. The parry serves to *deflect* the attack and not to push it away.

Fig. 7.33. Observe that the fencer on the right has shifted weight to the rear leg in an effort to avoid penetration, while the sword arm has dropped, opening the sixte line.

3. The fencer delivering the practice thrust must make a concerted effort to hit the target. One must ensure that his or her partner either parries correctly or is scored upon. This gives the parry a genuine opportunity to test itself. (See Fig. 7.33.) When delivering the thrust, the beginner will initially anticipate his or her partner's parry, causing the attack to intentionally veer away from the target. This habit must be given special instruction if practice is to be meaningful.

4. When the fencer feels that his or her attempt to score has been parried, the sword arm must relax instantly, which will allow for an easy return to guard in sixte. One must not stay in the lunge position, attempting to force a scoring touch through a successfully completed parry. Here sensitivity counts, and the beginner must learn to recognize when the attack has failed. The ability to attack with conviction, coupled with the sensitivity to know when to retreat, is an essential ingredient to fencing expertise. Partnership practice depends on this knowledge, as does fencing skill.

It is through alternating drills and partnership training that the best results are obtained. Each method of practice complements the other. The main prerequisite for learning during this crucial stage of instruction is patience. Defense is the most difficult aspect of fencing to learn, and the student must allow a good deal of time before he or she is able to assimilate all of its basic elements as outlined in this chapter. It will take many practice sessions and reviews before skill level reflects measurable improvement.

LOW-LINE PARRIES

It is best to practice the low-line parries of octave and septime after the high-line parries have been learned. (See Figs. 7.34 and 7.35.) The reason is that the low-line parries are more easily learned because of the carry-over from the learning process related to high-line parries. Also, we can assume that the fencer will have experienced informal bouting sessions with classmates and will feel a need for low-line instruction.

The methodology of the drills and partnership practice applies to low-line as well as to high-line instruction. However, there are technical differences worth noting.

When practicing low-line parries, thrusts are delivered to the lower area of the target, concentrating primarily on attacks to the outside or octave line. It is important to know that the vast majority of low-line attacks in modern fencing are aimed to the outside line under the arm, where the target area is larger than that offered by the inside line. The inside low-line target consists of only the groin area. Because of the torso posture while on guard, this small groin target becomes very difficult to hit even under the best of circumstances. Consequently the modern fencer finds it expedient to concentrate all low-line offensive action to the outside low line which is protected by the octave parry. (See Fig. 7.36.) The beginning fencer is well advised to know this. Low-

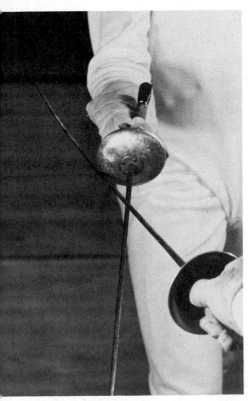

Fig. 7.34. Octave parry. The hand rolls outward to a supinated position while the blade tip is dropped to ensure a secure parry.

Fig. 7.35. Septime parry. Note that the hand maintains a supinated position while the tip of the blade is dropped to ensure a secure parry.

Fig. 7.36. The thrust to the octave low outside line. Note that the hand has rolled from the guard into a pronated position with the arm completely straight, the wrist slightly broken, and the foil blade bending securely into the target.

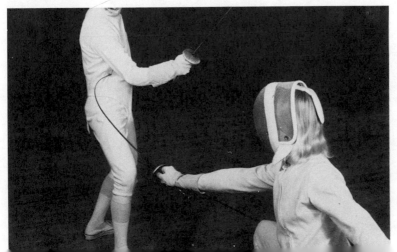

line parry practice should place prime emphasis on the octave parry. Septime parry is rarely used as a means of defense, because its function has been gradually taken over by the octave parry. Assuming the student is able to parry without losing his or her guard posture, the following points are of special importance to instruction.

a) When parrying either octave or septime, the point of the foil should not be lowered below the knee.

b) When parrying either octave or septime, the foil grip must not be allowed to roll inward. A supinated hand position is essentially the same for the low-line parries as that of the hand when in sixte.

c) When lowering the foil into the low-line parry positions, the sword arm must not extend or straighten out. When parrying septime or octave the sword-arm elbow will close the distance between itself and the right hip. To lower the foil one need only relax the shoulder, allowing the entire arm to drop a few inches. Observe this point carefully in Figs. 7.34 and 7.35.

Finally, fencers must continuously remind themselves that all parries are performed with *the arm well back in guard position*. When attacking, the arm should be fully extended. The fencer who insists on performing parries with a straight arm will simply find that progress is impossible.

CHAPTER 8

METHODS OF ATTACK

THE LUNGE

Any given attack can be delivered through any one of four different means, the lunge, the pattinando, the ballestra or the fleché. Of these the lunge is basic and by far the most important method of offensive scoring. The lunge is as basic to the attack as the guard is to the parry system. The fencer who is unwilling to spend the amount of time and energy it takes to develop a powerful lunge will have little offensive capability, even though he or she possesses a hundred attacks in his or her repertoire.

The lunge demands the most physical energy of all movements in fencing. One needs to have strong legs and much stamina. A four-minute fencing bout may require twenty lunges against a difficult opponent, where offensive action may be the only means of making a touch. The highly competitive fencer cannot afford a faulty lunge, and the beginning fencer must be prepared to work very hard if the lunge is to become an effective element of his or her game.

Purpose of the Lunge

The lunge is designed to deliver an attack instantly and without warning to the defender's target area and to allow time for a safe recovery in the event the effort fails. The dual purpose of the lunge offers the only sound approach to offensive action, for the modern fencer cannot afford to risk an attack which leaves him or her vulnerable to the defender's riposte.

Mechanics of the Lunge

The lunge begins with the powerful thrusting action of the rear leg, together with the rear arm which is forcefully thrown straight back and downward, creating an explosive forward movement of the body. This movement is led by a fully extended sword arm, which reaches with the tip of the foil for the earliest possible arrival on the target area. (See Fig. 8.1.) Coinciding with the extension of the sword arm, the front leg

Fig. 8.1. The arm extension (development). Note that the torso leans slightly forward from the hips up and that the legs remain well bent in preparation for the lunging action.

reaches straight forward in full extension, with the heel of the foot skimming the ground where it will finally come to rest. This allows the front leg to receive the forward momentum of the body, thus ending the lunge in a stable and balanced posture. (See Fig. 8.2.) A perfect lunge will leave the rear arm, the shoulders, the hips, and the right thigh level, paralleling the floor. The head will remain upright on top of the spine, which may lean slightly forward from its vertical posture during the guard. The front knee will rest directly above the heel, with the foot pointing forward. At this point, the fencer should be equally capable of recovering forward or backward to the guard position. Also, the torso and shoulders should be relaxed, giving full opportunity to continue fighting in the lunge position should this be necessary.

Fig. 8.2. The lunge. Observe the depth of the lunge; one may define a straight line from the right knee to the left foot. The torso is relaxed, leaning slightly forward, and the right knee rests directly over the right heel. The fencer's head remains upright, ensuring perfect vision.

THE RECOVERY

The recovery back to guard is easily performed by *pushing* back with the front leg while *pulling* back with the rear knee. Both legs work in unison to ensure that the recovery is completed back to a bent-knee guard position, rather than up and then down to the knee position. Recovering back to the up-guard position is a common error.

The forward recovery is easily accomplished by a slight lean forward and up to guard stance, with the rear foot moving into position last. This recovery feels quite natural and is easily mastered with limited instruction.

THE PATTINANDO

The pattinando is used against a defender who habitually retreats when attacked, making it impossible to score with the lunge. This move is essential to modern fencing because of the increased distance between the two fencers which is due to the faster pace of today's competition. The lunge simply does not travel far enough for all occasions.

Mechanics of the Pattinando

The pattinando is a marriage of the advance and lunge and is performed in one continuous sequence. For proper execution, the front foot steps forward as in the advance and is followed up at a sharply accelerated pace by the step of the rear foot, which instantly fires the lunge. From the opponent's point of view the pattinando looks like the beginning of a normal, cautious advance which is suddenly transformed into a lightning-fast attack. Not only does the pattinando outreach the lunge, but used properly it carries a tremendous element of surprise. Because of the momentum gained in the execution of the pattinando, it takes a strong lunge to control the power with which it finishes.

THE BALLESTRA

The ballestra is the most powerful method of attack and serves much the same purpose as the pattinando. The ballestra is designed for increased velocity during the attack. Where the pattinando combines the advance-lunge into one sequential action, the ballestra combines the properties of the jump-lunge.

Mechanics of the Ballestra [Cross-Bow]

The first stage of the ballestra consists of a jump which pushes off from the rear leg. As the front foot begins its step, the rear leg propels the fencer forward with a sharp, fast, jumping action. Both feet then land simultaneously, with the rear foot landing flat while only the ball of the front foot strikes the floor. Instantly, before weight can settle, the momentum of this specialized jump bounces the fencer into the most powerful lunge to be found in fencing.

THE FLECHÉ [ARROW]

The fleché is the only method of attack that does not depend on the lunge for success. The fleché is essentially a running action used in place of the lunge, pattinando, or ballestra. Beginners are more likely to fleché, for its execution is easily learned and performed. However, the fleché offers limited opportunity in varieties of attack and is best used to advantage as a surprise element. The main disadvantage of the fleché is that it offers no safe recovery other than running, and makes it impossible to defend against the riposte. While the fleché has its limitations, it is worthwhile if not overused. Beginners should never be encouraged to fleché. (See Figs. 8.3 and 8.4.)

Mechanics of the Fleché

From the guard position the sword arm is fully extended, and is accompanied by a strong forward lean of the torso; this places the fencer in a forward-moving, off-balance position with all of one's weight rolling over and supported by the front leg. At the extreme moment of forward commitment, the front leg pushes vigorously to propel the fencer toward the target. Regardless of whether the attack lands or misses, the fencer must continue in a run, passing to the right of his or her opponent, to regain balance. If the run is not continued, the fencer will most likely crash to the floor much to his or her own embarrassment and to the satisfaction of the opponent. The speed of the fleché limits attacks to simple feints and direct action.

PRACTICE

The lunge is the most difficult fencing technique to master. The beginner's legs are not prepared for the stretch, strain, and muscular demands

Fig. 8.3. The fleché. As the arm reaches to full extension, the body begins to roll forward, setting the right leg for the springing action which is to follow.

Figure 8.5. ▶

Fig. 8.4. Observe the total commitment of the fleché; the fencer forms a complete lay-out, creating a nearly straight line from the foil point to the left heel.

made by the lunge. The fencer must take sufficient time to adapt to this difficult posture, executing only a few lunges at first and working to increased numbers with each drill. With ten weeks practice, a fencer can be expected to lunge to exhaustion without developing stiff legs or the general muscular discomfort associated with the first lunging attempts. The lunge should be practiced *slowly* at the start, ensuring that each of its component parts is done correctly. The beginner will find it most difficult to hold a balanced lunge and impossible to recover to the correct guard position. However, with methodical practice these difficulties will disappear as legs strengthen. Eventually the fencer can expect lunges delivered smoothly with full-arm extension leading the way and recoveries that return to perfect guard position. A common error is failure to place equal emphasis on the recovery. Patience and an eye to the future are needed if success in this difficult area of fencing is to be gained.

The pattinando should be added to the repertoire when the lunge appears to develop stability. This can normally be expected around the fifth week of practice. The ballestra is considered an advanced technique and should only be introduced after a reasonable command of the pattinando has been established.

The fleché should not be used by beginners. If it becomes necessary to introduce the fleché to one's game, it should be used with the clear understanding that it must not replace the lunge.

The techniques of the lunge, pattinando, and ballestra are nicely integrated into mobility sessions. Combining methods of attack with footwork adds interest to drills and presents the fencer with challenging alternatives. For example: advance, retreat, lunge; advance, advance, lunge; retreat, advance, pattinando; retreat, retreat, advance, ballestra! The combinations are limitless.

ATTACKS

The attack is defined as the "initial offensive action executed by extending the arm and continuously threatening the opponent's valid surface (target)."* There are countless methods of attack which involve differing preparation, such as feints and beats. For every attack there

---

*A.F.L.A. Rules Book, p. 14.

exists a defense, and it is evident that fencers must have at their disposal a variety of offensive actions if they are to succeed in penetrating their opponent's parry system.

The beginner, having acquired reasonable skill in the guard, footwork, lunge, and basic parry positions, must now learn how to deliver an offensive action. He or she is faced with the problem of deciding which attacks should be studied first. *Beginning attacks should embody all of the essentials of basic understanding and technique which will allow the fencer an easier progression to more advanced attack methodology.* It is with this consideration in mind that the following list of attacks has been prepared. It is recommended that they be learned in the order in which they are presented.

Fig. 8.6. The direct attack.

Basic Attacks

1. *The direct attack to high line.* The student should be familiar with the *direct attack* through his or her practice in learning the lunge and

parry positions. This is the simplest of all attacks and is performed by extending the arm, threatening the target, and lunging directly from guard position to the proposed target area. The direct attack should be executed as one smooth, continuous movement; it arrives with the point of the weapon fasted securely on the target and with the blade bending upward just enough to ensure a valid touch. (See Fig. 8.6.) The attack should end in a perfect lunge, allowing for an easy recovery back to the guard position.

2. *The beat-direct attack to high line.* The beat-direct attack is performed by executing a strong, crisp beat to the *medium* of the opponent's blade as preparation for a lightning-fast extension and lunge to the target. The beat is used as a surprise element, momentarily disrupting the opponent's ability to respond with a parry.

It must be observed that both the direct and beat-direct attacks depend completely upon the element of surprise if they are to score before the defender has a chance to parry. They are the least difficult of all attacks to defend against, and successful execution depends on perfect timing, distance, and speed.

3. *Feint attacks.* The *feint attack* is used against an opponent who has proven he or she will parry a direct attack. The only sure method of obtaining this proof is to try a direct attack. If it fails because the opponent has parried, one has positive information upon which to try a feint. The objective of the feint attack is to threaten the opponent's line with a full extension of the sword arm, creating the impression that a direct attack is in progress. Then the defender, receiving the split-second impression that he or she is being threatened, attempts to parry. The attacking blade is then manipulated to deceive the attempted parry with a "disengage"* by passing under and around the parry and continuing forward to the target with completion of the lunge.

The feint attack depends upon perfect execution if it is to be successful. It must constitute an actual threat to the defender's target. The feint and disengage-lunge must be coordinated as one forward attacking movement which gains velocity from begining to end and which terminates with the point reaching the target at maximum speed and power.

---

*When used with feints, the disengage implies that the attacking blade passes under and around the defender's blade from one line to another.

Fig. 8.7. The feint into quarte line. Note that the arm is fully extended, placing a direct threat to the inside high line.

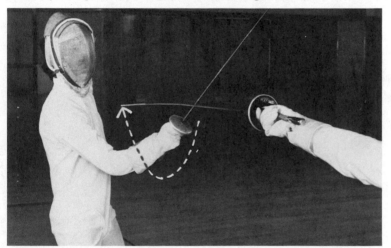

Fig. 8.8. The disengage. The disengage is performed with a fully extended arm, employing the fingers (manipulators) and hand for blade manipulation.

Fig. 8.9. The hit. Observe the blade bending into the target, fastening the touch securely so that it does not slip off or pass by.

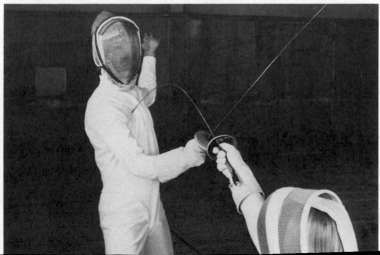

There are four feint attacks with which the beginner should be familiar:

a) The straight feint. The attack feints into the opponent's quarte line straight from the guard position, disengaging and scoring into the open sixte line which is created by the defender's attempt to parry the feint. (See Figs. 8.7, 8.8, and 8.9.)

b) The feint sixte disengage. The attacking blade passes from guard position under the defender's blade, feinting into the sixte line, disengaging, and scoring into the quarte line. (See Figs. 8.10, 8.11, and 8.12.)

Fig. 8.10. Feint sexte disengage. Observe on the feint that the hand remains in a supinated position and that the point reaches deeply into the sixte line.

Fig. 8.11. Observe the line of the disengage, which passes under and around the defender's forearm as the arm continues its reach toward the target.

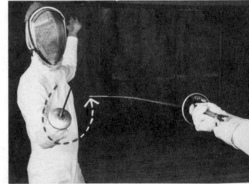

Fig. 8.12. Observe the blade hooking into and on the target, ensuring a firm touch.

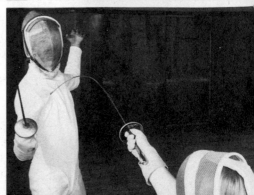

c) Feint low-high. The attack feints into the defender's low outside line, drawing an octave or second parry response, and disengages vertically up and around the outside line, scoring to the defender's exposed high line. (See Figs. 8.13, 8.14, and 8.15.)

d) Feint double disengage (designated as a "one-two" by many fencing teachers). The double disengage incorporates two disengages which are designed to deceive a defense where two parries are executed in combination, preventing the single disengage attack from scoring. The fencer must keep in mind that the lunge always *accompanies the final disengage* of attacks in which multiple disengages are used.

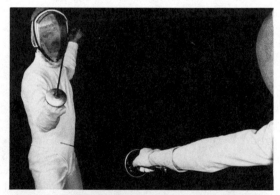

Fig. 8.13. Feint low-high. Observe the full extension of the arm with the hand in a pronated position and the wrist slightly broken, placing the blade in line with the target and parallel to the floor.

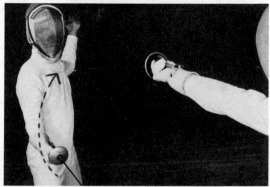

Fig. 8.14. Observe that as the blade disengages upward the arm continues its reach toward the high-line target.

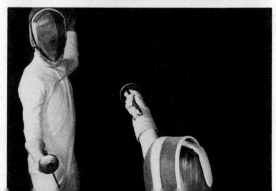

Fig. 8.15. Observe that the point lands with the blade hooking into the high-line target.

4. *Beat disengage attacks.* The beat is used for the same purpose as the feint. The beat is designed to draw a parry response from the opponent, creating an opportunity to score with a disengage lunge to the open line which results from the defender's parry reaction. The beat should be powerful and crisp, avoiding all grazing contact which results from sloppy execution. The disengage must occur instantly off the beat, while the arm simultaneously extends, directing the foil to the opened line as the lunge carries the point to the target.

There are three basic beat disengage attacks which are practical for the beginning fencer to learn.

a) Beat quarte, disengage. An attack that prepares by beating the opponent's blade in quarte line, disengages, and scores into the sixte line.

b) Beat sixte, disengage. An attack which prepares by beating into the sixte line, disengages, and scores into the quarte line.

c) Beat quarte, double disengage. An attack executed against a defense that consists of two consecutive high-line parries (quarte, sixte), thus preventing the beat single disengage from scoring. Here the fencer beats in quarte and instantly performs two disengages, deceiving both the quarte and sixte parry responses of the defender.

5. *Direct attack to low line.* This attack is most useful against opponents who have a weak low-line defense. Introducing this attack to beginning fencers provides an excellent motivation for them to develop their low line parries.*

To execute the low-line attack the fencer extends to the octave or outside line, aiming the foil at the target area under the sword arm and above the right hip. This is then instantly followed through with a lunge. (See Figs. 8.16 and 8.17.) Note that the arm extension is low, which places the hand on a line parallel to the target area. While performing the extension, the hand is rolled into a pronated position with the fingers down. The angle between the blade, which extends parallel to

---

*It is not advisable to concentrate on low-line attacks until an ability to perform high-line attacks has been demonstrated. The beginner has a natural tendency to fall low on all attacks and must not be encouraged in this habit through formal instruction in low-line strategy.

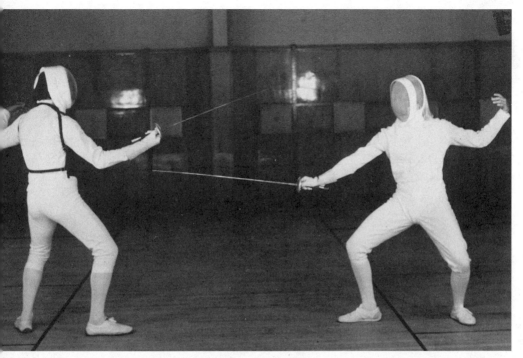

Fig. 8.16. Development of the low-line attack.

Fig. 8.17. The lunge to low line.

the floor, and the arm-extension is created by a slight break in the wrist. Note in Fig. 8.17 that *the blade bends outward, hooking into the target and ensuring firm penetration for the touch.*

While the attacks presented in this chapter do not comprise the total number of attacks available to the fencer, they do form a sound basis for instruction and practice for the first-year fencer. The fencer who can perform these attacks will have little difficulty learning innovations and new varieties of offensive action.

Advanced Attacks

When a sound understanding of basic attacks has been established, the fencer is ready for more advanced offensive thinking. It is important to know as many attacks as possible, even though one may use only a few on any single opponent. What works against one adversary may not be effective against another. If the student can acquire a versatile repertoire of offensive action, it becomes relatively easy to recognize what other fencers are doing. It is essential that the fencer recognize attacks as they are used by his or her adversary, for in this way one can easily find the right defense to use when the situation grows difficult. The fencer who does not know the means by which his or her opponent scores is certain to be hit again. The following attacks are basic to the advanced fencer's technique. Again, this list by no means pretends to cover the infinite variations of offensive strategy available to the fencer. It will, however, clarify the broad base from which all fencers must draw in the creation of their personal offensive technique.

The coupé (cut over). The coupé is used in place of the disengage. After a feint or beat preparation the blade is brought back, tip upward, and passes over the tip of the defender's blade, resuming its forward thrusting movement into the opposite line of preparation. (See Figs. 8.18 through 8.20.) The upward motion of the blade is performed by breaking the *wrist* and *elbow* slightly, with just enough backward motion to clear the length of the defender's blade. The coupé must continue from the beating or feinting preparation as one continuous movement ending in the extension and lunge to the target. The coupé is an excellent method of attack against all parry systems and is used by most fencers. However, a word of warning: The coupé is vulnerable to stop thrusts, and its overuse is certain to weaken one's offensive game.

The beat coupé to low line. This is an easily executed attack and one of the most effective low-line strategies. Here the attack is prepared by a

Fig. 8.18. The feint.

Fig. 8.19. The coupé. The blade is withdrawn only as far as necessary to clear the defender's foil tip. Also, observe that the coupé is performed by the combined flexing of the arm and wrist.

Fig. 8.20. The completion of the coupé places the point into scoring lines.

sharp beat in quarte which is instantly followed through with a coupé thrust directly into the octave or outside low-line target. The beat coupé action is done as one fluid and powerful motion which rounds off with the hand in a pronated position to ensure that the blade hooks into the low-line target, scoring approximately ten inches below the defender's armpit. This is an excellent attack which is not vulnerable to stop thrusts once the beat has been established. The preparation for this attack requires sufficient distance and excellent timing if the beating action is to be successful. When properly executed, it is a most difficult attack to parry and must be included in any advanced repertoire.

The beat sixte coupé. Here the beat and the coupé are combined to draw a sixte reaction opening the quarte or inside high-line. The attack prepares with a beat coupé in sixte which transfers the attacking blade over and into the defender's quarte line for the scoring touch. The beat coupé must be performed very fast as one fluid and powerful movement ending in a lunge or fleché. This attack lends itself beautifully to the timing of a fleché and is recommended especially to small fencers who find difficulty in reaching the target of tall fencers.

Beat-coupé disengage. This attack is executed in the same manner as the beat coupé, except that the attacker adds the disengage as a tactic against the defender who can manage a quarte parry. If the beat coupé fails, try the beat coupé disengage on the next offensive opportunity. These two attacks are excellent complements to each other. By alternating them one may score many touches that cannot be gained otherwise.

Multiple coupés. Just as the fencer can use multiple disengages, two or more coupés can be used successfully to create a scoring opportunity. However, the fencer must not make a habit of offensive action based on this type of attack. The stop thrust was designed for use against the coupé. The fencers who get hung up on coupé attacks (which happens frequently because of their effectiveness and ease in application on the lower levels of fencing) will find themselves with a habit that will only lead to defeat on the higher levels of fencing. The coupé is the most easily defeated attack in fencing through use of the "reliant" stop thrust.

The direct insistence. This is one of the most powerful attacks in fencing as far as muscular strength and velocity is concerned. The object is to attack directly into the closed sixte line with such surprise and force that the line is forced open, allowing the point to score. The attack literally insists its way through the guard. The insistence is designed to take unexpected advantage of an opponent whose attention has lapsed or who has a weak sixte parry. (See Figs. 8.21 and 8.22.)

Fig. 8.21. The insistence. Observe the thrust, which is placed with a powerful lateral pressure against the blade in sixte line.

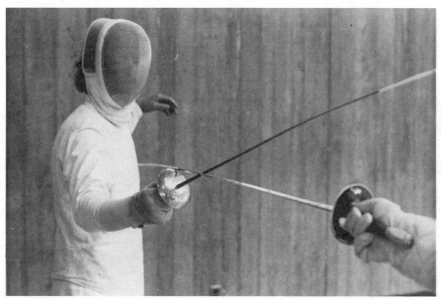

Fig. 8.22. Observe that the guard is forced out of line as the scoring touch arrives.

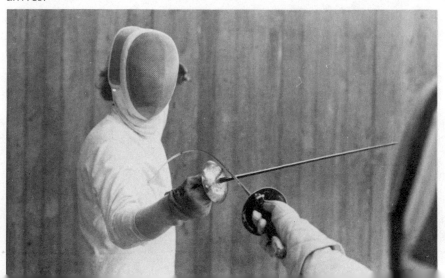

The insistence disengage. This is an excellent attack best used against the heavy-handed fencer who parries with a strong sixte reaction and who cannot be hit with a direct insistence. Here a powerful insisting thrust is placed against the medium of the defender's blade. As the defender responds to the pressure of the insistence, the attacker releases the blade by disengaging and lunges into the inside quarte line which has been opened by the defender's compulsive sixte reaction. (See Figs. 8.23 through 8.25.)

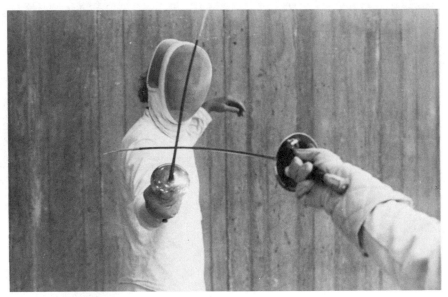

Fig. 8.23. The insistence is done powerfully to draw a strong sixte response from the opponent.

The insistence coupé. This attack is prepared in essentially the same way as the insistence disengage. Instead of disengaging, the insistence is followed through with a powerful backward coupé action which maintains blade contact until it passes over the defender's blade, and thrusts into the opened quarte line. The insistence coupé is executed as one continuous action and is best performed with the pattinando or ballestra.

Insistence quarte direct. This insistence is used to draw an octave response. Here the attacker extends forcefully, exerting pressure on the

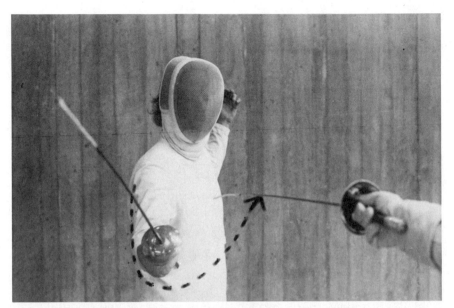

Fig. 8.24. At the instant of response the disengage is performed.

Fig. 8.25. The attack is brought to completion by the lunge.

top of the defender's blade in quarte, which conveys the impression that the attack is forcing its way toward the octave line. As the defender reacts with a ceding parry to octave, the attacking blade is instantly directed straight to the high line and is delivered by the completion of the lunge. The insistence, extension, and lunge must be performed as one continuous action which gains speed until the scoring touch is made. This attack is best performed with the ballestra. However, it can also be executed using the pattinando.

The coulé (glide). In contrast to the strength of the insistence, the coulé places a light grazing action on the defender's blade which is also designed to draw a parry response. As with the insistence, the coulé is best directed into the sixte line and should combine a feint with the grazing action on the blade. Here the attack is prepared by thrusting lightly *on* and *along* the defender's blade with the point of the blade aiming as closely as possible toward the sixte line. The defender should *see* and *feel* the threat. As a parry response is made, the attack disengages, scoring into the quarte line. The coulé is a sensitive attack requiring skill and lightness of touch. It must be performed smoothly with the grazing action of the threat continuing into the disengage as one complete movement to the target.

The doublé (circular attack). The doublé is a deceiving offensive action with the blade designed to evade the defensive action of circular parries. Normally, the doublé is preceded by a feint which is designed to trigger a circular parry. The feint is followed by a circular movement of the point which travels over, around, and through the circular defense on its way to the target. When the doublé is used against a circular sixte parry it rotates counterclockwise, and when used against the circular quarte parry the rotation is clockwise. The component parts of the doublé attack, the feint, circulation of the point, and lunge should be executed as one continuous forward movement. The point of the foil, in effect, corkscrews its way through the defender's movement.

Opposition attack to octave. The opposition attack is used most effectively against the fencer who fences with an extended arm, which places the blade within reaching distance of the attacker. The object of the opposition attack is to gain control of the defender's blade during the entire course of the offensive, thus preventing a possibility for the defender to parry. Here the attack is delivered *on and in opposition to*

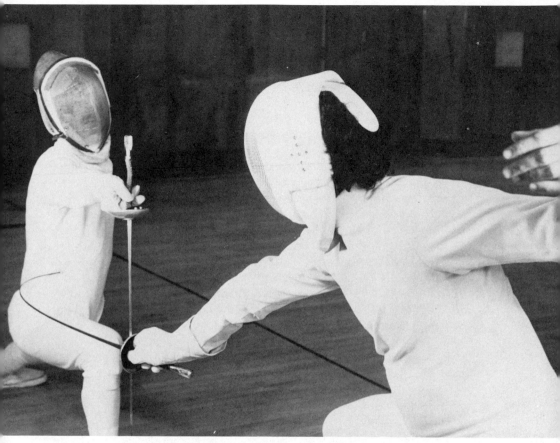

Fig. 8.26. Note that, unlike the direct insistence, which forces the line open with strong blade action, the opposition attack dominates the blade with the guard, which is held in pronation.

the opponent's blade, using the guard to push it aside simultaneously with the scoring thrust of the offensive action. (See Fig. 8.26.)

The press disengage. The press is used to the same effect as the beat, in that it is designed to draw a parry response. Because the press can only be done from an engaged position, the fencer's first task is to create blade contact. Once engagement has been achieved, the fencer initiating the attack simply needs to press the *medium* of the opponent's blade *sharply* to draw a parry reaction. Once this response is made the attacker disengages and lunges to the open line. The press must be done cleanly without slipping or grazing blades. A good press will feel like the sudden smooth jerk of a fish biting on the line. The press can have a startling effect when done by surprise and will usually draw a sharp parry reaction. Because modern fencers seldom fence from an engaged position, the press is rarely seen, as it requires careful preparation to set up. However, the smart fencer can always find opportunities to use the press. It is a good attack to keep in mind.

The froissé. The froissé is the single most powerful preparation for attack in fencing. It is the only technique specifically designed to disarm one's opponent. The froissé is executed as a powerful, sharp, forward-striking action against the weak of the blade in the defender's sixte line. The movement of the froissé is forward, causing a binding force against the defender's blade which is followed through with a full extension and lunge as one continuous direct attack. (See Figs. 8.27, 8.28 and 8.29.) The attack must arrive as a distinct continuation of the froissé and not as a second separate movement. The rules will allow a touch against a disarmed opponent only when it scores simultaneously with the disarming.

Fig. 8.27. Observe the blade placed in preparation for the froissé, where it may strike into the sixte line to the weak of the defender's blade.

Fig. 8.28. At the instant of disarming, the attacking blade is found aiming directly into the sixte line.

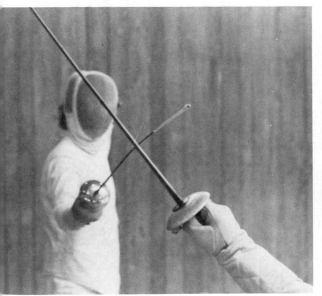

The froissé must not be overused for effectiveness. It must always be a surprise, for it cannot be performed against an alert opponent. However, there are moments when one's adversary will forget, allowing the froissé its opportunity.

The bind. The bind is a forceful offensive action against the opponent's blade which transfers the defending blade from one line of defense to another. The bind is used as a means to energetically disrupt the opponent's defense long enough to create a scoring advantage. The bind is executed by gaining control of the defending blade with the medium of the attacking blade while vigorously sweeping it from one line to another. To be effective, the bind must be executed from a relatively close distance from which blade contact can be made. The pattinando and ballestra are most effective as a means of closing distance in preparation for the bind. The bind depends on speed, power, and a complete surprise element for effectiveness. The fencer must be aware of the danger of stop thrusts, in the event that the defender's blade is not found while attempting a binding preparation for the attack. (See Figs. 8.30, 8.31 and 8.32.)

Fig. 8.29. The froissé extension ending in the lunge.

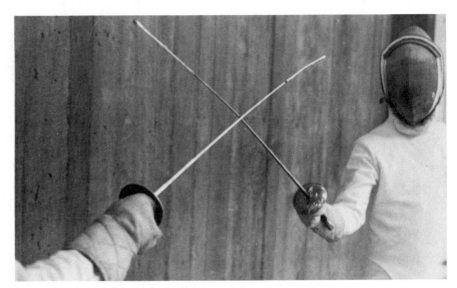

Fig. 8.30. The bind. Observe that blade contact is made at the medium of the blades.

Fig. 8.31. The bind is made by a sharp and powerful whipping movement.

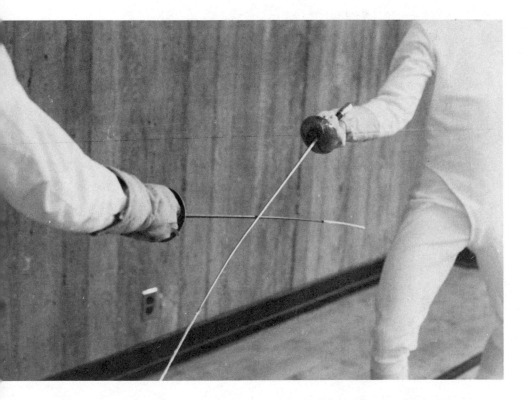

Fig. 8.32. The opponent's blade is forced at the completion of the bind to the opposite diagonally located line, from sixte to septime

The envelopment. The envelopment is executed in much the same manner as the bind. However, where the bind transfers the defending blade from one line to another, the envelopment transfers the blade completely around in a circular movement, returning it to the original line in which blade contact was initiated. Having disrupted the opponent's defense, the attacker should be able to score to the target. Like the bind, the envelopment is sparingly used in modern fencing because of the difficulty in its execution. Failure to find the blade in an attempted envelopment leaves the attacker subject to the stop thrust. The envelopment can only find success through excellent timing, speed, and power. The envelopment is easily parried through the use of ceding parries. (See Figs. 8.33, 8.34 and 8.35.)

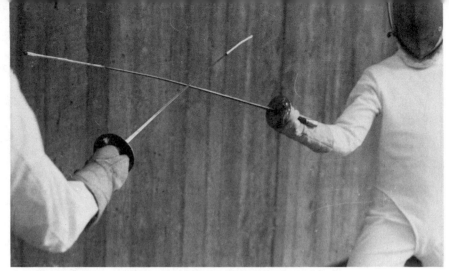

Fig. 8.33. The envelopment. Medium engagement is made as with the bind.

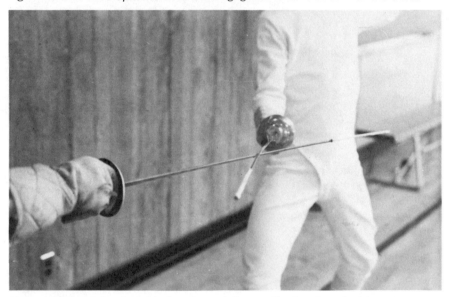

Fig. 8.34. The defender's blade is forced diagonally downward with a binding action.

Fig. 8.35. The action completes itself as one continuous movement back at the original engagement position.

CHAPTER 9

THE RIPOSTE AND COUNTERATTACKS

As we previously stated, defense begins with a sound parry system. It must also be stated that the parry serves to create counteroffensive techniques which are as important to defense as the parry itself. The parry can create situations in which other means of scoring are made possible. The *riposte, counter-parry,* * *counter-riposte,* and *remise* are all vital techniques which are inseparable from the parry system.

THE RIPOSTE

The riposte can be defined as any attempt to score which is initiated by the defender after the completion of a successful parry. The riposte is designed to score by catching the opponent before or during the recovery from an attack which has been parried. All fencers are vulnerable during the instant when their attack has met with failure.

There are four classifications of ripostes: the direct riposte, the indirect riposte, the delayed riposte, and the counter-riposte.

---

*The terms "counter-parry" and "circular parry" are used synonymously by many fencing authorities. A strict definition of these terms is used in this book for purposes of clarification.

The Direct or "Simple" Riposte

To be effective the direct riposte must be delivered instantly upon completion of the parry. The trained fencer will never permit his or her opponent the privilege of recovering from an attack without the necessity of defending himself or herself from a deadly and well-timed riposte. The direct riposte scores to the same line as that of the parry. For example, when parrying quarte, the riposte scores to the attacker's quarte or high inside line. (See Figs. 9.1, 9.2, 9.3.) When parrying sixte, the riposte scores to the high outside or sixte line. (See Figs. 9.4, 9.5, and 9.6.) When parrying octave, the riposte scores to the low outside or octave line. (See Figs. 9.7, 9.8, and 9.9.)

The Counter-Parry

All parries that are used to defend against ripostes are *counter-parries*. The counter-parry may be performed at the completion of a parried attack, during the recovery from the lunge, or in the guard position against a counter-riposte. In all instances *the counter-parry is the prime defense against the riposte.* A riposte which is delivered from a counter-parry is a *counter-riposte*. It is during exchanges involving parries, ripostes, counter-parries, and counter-ripostes that the fencer's skill is most severely tested. The lightning-fast speed at which this interaction takes place readily exposes errors in technique.

The Indirect or "Compound" Riposte

The indirect riposte incorporates all of the features of the direct riposte, except that it scores to the opposite line in which the parry has been made. It is used against the fencer who parries a direct riposte. The indirect riposte deceives the opponent's attempted parry by means of the disengage. For example, after parrying quarte the blade is instantly dropped low enough to allow the quarte counter-parry to pass over it and is then delivered to the exposed sixte line. (See Figs. 9.10, 9.11, 9.12, 9.13.) When parrying sixte, the blade is dropped under the opponent's counter-parry of sixte and delivered to the exposed quarte line. Against opponents who defend with combination counter-parries one may perform the double or triple disengage ripostes. For every counter-parry the opponent places in the path of the riposte, there must be one disengage. The simple disengage is frequently used in fencing, because most advanced-level fencers can parry a direct riposte. The double disengage is used infrequently, and the triple disengage is used rarely. The more complex the riposte the more vulnerable one becomes to the remise.

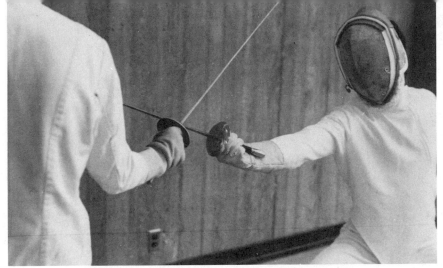

Fig. 9.1. The direct quarte riposte. The attack is parried in quarte.

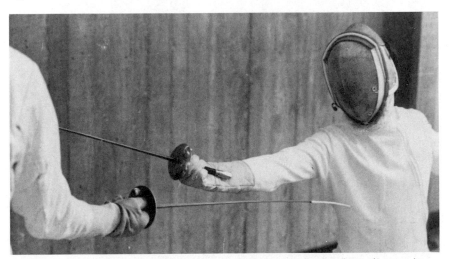

Fig. 9.2. Observe that the riposting blade is instantly dropped into line on its way to the target.

Fig. 9.3. The riposte arrives to the broad, flat midsection of the opponent's target, where it has the best chance to score without accidentally hitting off-target to the arm or mask.

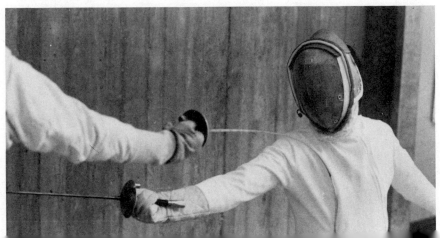

Fig. 9.4. The direct sixte riposte. The attack is parried in sixte.

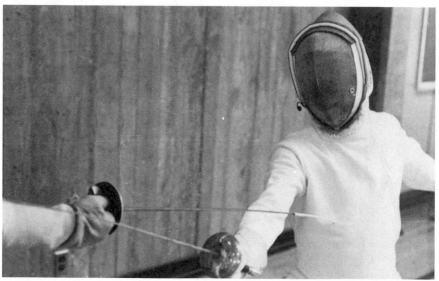

Fig. 9.5. The riposting blade is instantly dropped into line.

Fig. 9.6. The riposte completes itself, scoring to the chest of the opponent.

Fig. 9.7. The attack to the outside low line is parried in octave.

Fig. 9.8. The riposting blade is brought into line with the guard in pronation.

Fig. 9.9. Note that as the riposte scores, the blade bends into the target for good penetration.

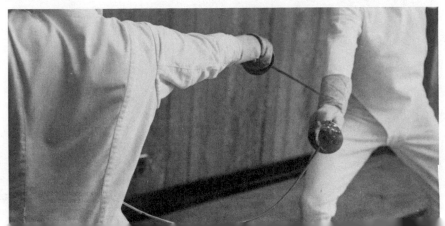

Fig. 9.10. The attack is parried in quarte.

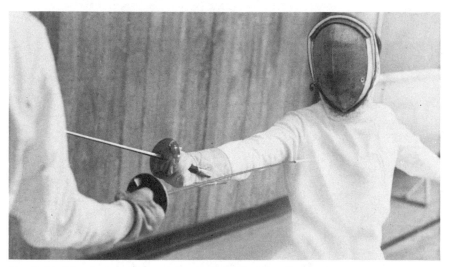

Fig. 9.11. The riposte drops to line as it begins the disengage.

Fig. 9.12. The disengaging action, having completed itself by passing under the opponent's attempt to defend with a counter quarte parry, is now ready to score to the sixte line.

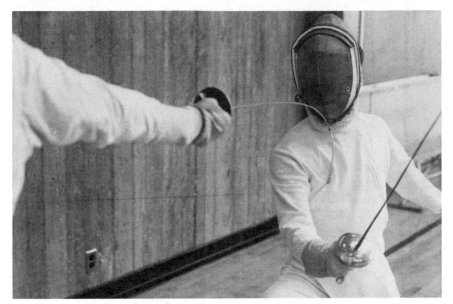

Fig. 9.13. The riposte completes itself, scoring to the sixte line. The entire sequence should take about one second.

The Delayed Riposte

All parries may be held in place (holding parry) for a tempo or two, delaying the release of the riposte. The delayed riposte can have a disconcerting effect on the fencer who expects to receive and is prepared for an immediate riposte response. The holding action which delays the riposte is used to break the attacker's fencing rhythm or tempo, causing a short-circuiting of his or her reaction patterns. This creates a lapse in his or her ability to parry which may last for only a second but which allows the riposte ample time to score once it is released.

The delayed riposte is also used to time the moment of release for the best scoring advantage. Some fencers are hit easily at the conclusion of their attack, while others display defensive weakness during some stage of the recovery back to guard. The experienced fencer knows when the riposte can be used to advantage and will time it accordingly.

The Remise

The remise constitutes an instant replacement or renewal of attack, after an attack or riposte has failed in its attempt to score. The remise is used exclusively against the defender who delays the riposte or compulsively performs complex indirect counter action. The remise is a renewal of attack which must score before the defender can effect a riposte. The direct riposte is the answer to a fencer who compulsively remises. It should be noted that the beginning fencer, whose reaction patterns are not well formulated, will remise in place of parrying as an instinctive reaction. This tendency in beginners to abandon the proper sequence of the fencing phrase is a common error and should be avoided. Every effort should be made to use the remise selectively and in the proper situation. When in doubt, *parry.*

COUNTERATTACKS

The defender need not always parry. The counterattack is used in place of the parry as a form of defense which attacks into the opponent's offensive preparation. Successful fencers will *never* permit their adversaries knowledge of whether they will defend or attack. If one's adversary cannot count on a consistent defensive reaction, an offensive strategy is most difficult to plan. It is through the alternation of parries and counterattacks that the defender injects uncertainty into the adversary's offensive plans.

Counterattacks may be grouped into three convenient categories: the stop thrust, the time thrust, and the attack into tempo. Counterattacks are an essential and integral aspect of effective fencing technique. The fencer who fails to comprehend the importance and nature of counteroffensive technique is certain to suffer failure at the hands of one who does.

Stop Thrusts

The stop thrust is used to best advantage against the attacker who makes himself or herself vulnerable by carelessly rushing forward during the preparation of the attack, or who executes a faulty attack which fails to threaten the defender's target. In either case the defender is not obliged to parry. Rather, he or she may employ a stop thrust as a means of defense.

The stop thrust is performed by placing the point in line, with the arm fully extended, allowing the oncoming adversary to impale himself. The move must be exceptionally well-timed, catching the attacker before he or she is able to establish right-of-way; it must *score* before the final movement of the attack. The rules state that fencers who use the stopping action do so at their own risk. If the attack and the stop thrust arrive simultaneously, causing both fencers to be scored upon, there is a strong chance that the touch will be awarded against the defender who used the stopping action in place of the parry. Most officials are inclined to give the benefit of the doubt to actions which are in keeping with the fencing phrase. The stop thrust always breaks the phrase and so must be used judiciously. The experienced fencer will resort to the stop thrust only when it is appropriate and when it is certain that the officials will acknowledge its validity. This stands in contrast to the beginner, who always overuses stopping action out of a fear that his or her parry system isn't strong. When in doubt, *parry*.

There are two broad classifications of stop thrusts: the direct stop and the indirect stop (derobement).

The direct stop. As described above, the direct stop thrust is performed by simply extending the sword arm directly from guard position and holding the point in line until the attackers have impaled themselves. (See Fig. 9.14.)

Fig. 9.14. The direct stop. Observe that the stop thrust is delivered with energy and . conviction and that the legs are bent and firmly set.

The indirect stop (*derobement*). This stopping action is executed against the fencer who habitually beats, binds, or wrestles on the defending blade during preparation of the attack. Through disengagement the defender deceives the attacker's attempt to make blade contact by placing the point in line, thus allowing the impalement to take place.

The In Quartata [Quarter Turn]

The in quartata can be used directly or indirectly. It is specifically useful against the fencer who attacks fast and straight, and it is not restricted in its use to fencers who exhibit faulty preparation. The in quartata is named for its quarter side-step backward, which removes the defender's target area from the line of attack, thus dodging a potential scoring hit. (See Fig. 9.15.)

The dodging movement and the point extended into line must be done simultaneously, forcing the attacking adversary to impale himself or herself.

Fig. 9.15. The in quartata. Observe that the fencer steps backward, pivoting on the forward foot with most of the body weight on the rear leg.

Fig. 9.16. The passata sotto.

The Passata-Sotto

The passata-sotto executes the stop hit in coordination with a dodging movement as does the in quartata. However, where the in quartata side-steps, the passata-sotto ducks under the line of attack. (See Fig. 9.16.) As the attacker initiates, the defender drops quickly to the floor while placing the point in line, forcing the attack to *pass over* his or her body.

It is important to observe the form of the passata-sotto. As the fencer drops, he or she reaches to the floor, lending momentum to the downward movement. As he or she lands, the rib cage and the thigh of the right leg come into firm contact. The object is for the fencer to position himself or herself as low as possible without losing control of the foil, which is placed firmly forward for the impaling finale of the movement.

The Knee Drop

The knee drop serves the identical purpose of the passata-sotto but employs a squatting posture as its means to duck the attack. The knee drop is easily performed, but it does not reduce the target area as effectively as the passata-sotto. Many fencers prefer the knee drop to the passata-sotto because it is a relatively instinctive movement, requiring little training for execution. The knee drop is the lazy man's passata-sotto and should be avoided by the serious fencer, who may assure better results through mastery of the passata-sotto.

The Time Thrust

The time thrust is a stop thrust which blocks the line of attack simultaneously with the extension of the stopping action. (See Fig. 9.17.) To be effective in the time thrust, the fencer must anticipate

Fig. 9.17. The time thrust.

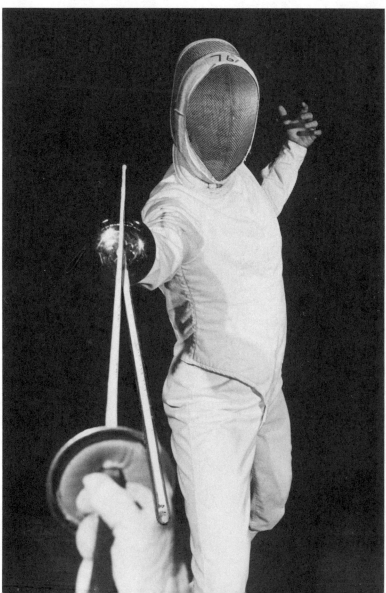

correctly the line in which the attack will be directed. The time thrust is infrequently used in modern fencing because of the difficulty in its technical execution. The slightest error spells disaster. This most advanced technique combines the defensive action of the parry with the striking immediacy of the stop thrust. When used successfully the time hit is virtually impossible to defend against, once one is caught in its trap. The beginner is advised to learn all basic techniques before seriously attempting this one.

Attack into Tempo

Like the direct stop thrust, the attack into tempo is executed against the attacker's initiation. The essential difference is that this stopping action is performed with a lunge. As one's adversary moves forward to prepare the attack, the defender lunges directly into the forward movement, catching the attacker before his or her plan can develop. The attack into tempo may be delivered to either the high or low line and may be prepared by a feint or beat, depending on the circumstances and the skill of one's opponent. Normally a direct action is sufficient if one's timing is correct.

Fig. 10.1. A fencer performs a reconnaissance engagement on the adversary's blade, seeking information which can be of tactical value.

CHAPTER 10

THE PSYCHOLOGY OF PRACTICE AND TACTICS

When one has gained sufficient technique and skill to engage in systematic sparring sessions, a most interesting challenge to one's learning process will reveal itself. The fencer soon discovers that the step from theory to practice is longer than first imagined. It becomes evident that one may know *how* and *when* to execute a specific action, but to actually effect it against a real and uncooperative adversary is a far different matter. Most fencers agree that the bridge between fencing theory and practice is the most fascinating speculation relative to the sport.

When practicing a specific action such as a parry or lunge in a noncompetitive training session, technique is easy to perform. However, when confronted with an aggressive sparring situation the simplest movements are suddenly transformed into clumsy, awkward gestures that can hardly be identified. When fencing for points, this separate reality soon becomes frustratingly apparent. The reason for this change is not difficult to understand, but its implications are far-reaching and of crucial importance to the fencer's development. It is well worth every serious fencer's time and effort to examine the issue thoughtfully.

Every beginning fencer *hates* to be scored against out of a fear of losing or humiliation. In a frantic effort not to lose, emotions take over, causing the individual to overreact and become rigid. In this state of nervous excitement, relaxed, fluid, economic movement is not possible.

PSYCHOLOGY OF TECHNIQUE

The first major reality the fencer must accept is that winning is not always a central issue. It is the distaste for losing which prevents well-executed technique even in low-pressured recreational sparring circumstances. The fencer must learn to temper ego involvement. He must good-naturedly accept touches against himself as part of the learning experience if sparring practice is to be a genuinely constructive experience.

When sparring, it is of paramount importance that the fencer learn to control his or her mental disposition, preventing overreactions to the aggressive demands of the opponent. Otherwise he or she will enter into a frenzy of panic-stricken thrusts and jabs which abandon all sensible approaches to a real scoring advantage. Or the opposite reaction may result: one may withdraw into a defensive shell, rooted to the floor in a state of near shock, where the most rudimentary fencing techniques become impossible to perform. Regardless of whether a compulsive reaction is offensive or defensive, it will mean certain defeat when fencing against an opponent who maintains true mental balance.

Psychological Balance

Everyone who fences has experienced this initial reaction to the unique competitive pressure that fencing creates. It is by overcoming the tendency to overreact that the fencer discovers a path to skilled execution of techniques which produce satisfactory scoring results. The fencer is ultimately training to achieve a *mental balance under pressure*, where a free use of offensive and defensive strategies becomes possible. Mental balance provides the only means by which the fencer can effectively respond to the lightning-fast offensive and defensive demands of a skilled opponent. It is from mental balance that the fencer gains the capability to release at a split-second notice a totally aggressive or totally defensive answer to an opponent's intentions. This balanced view is not victimized by its own aggressive or defensive energy but rather uses these energy polarities freely, according to the dictates of a given situation. In other words, the fencer learns to control his or her energy, releasing it only when it appears to be an effective means to a scoring advantage. Failing to do so wastes energy, leaving the fencer exhausted, frustrated, and defeated after only a few minutes of play.

Psychology of Sparring

Sparring sessions offer the conscientious fencer the best opportunity to practice mental balance, control of energy, and perfection of technique while fencing for actual touches. If one's mental state is too defensive, parries will overreact to the adversary's slightest offensive movements, while attacks will be difficult to perform and at best ill-timed. If one's mental state is overly aggressive, the parry system will be heavy-handed and insensitive, while the attacks will waste energy, lack point control, and score on everything but the opponent's target. Each fencer must use the sparring session as a means to fencing self-discovery. It is here that negative habits and technique are exposed and corrected for tactical advantage.

The changing nature of fencing interaction demands that the mental disposition of each fencer be flexible and ready to formulate new tactics at a moment's notice. With each scoring touch the strategy of the bout changes, for it is unlikely that one may score against an aware opponent twice in succession with the same action. For this reason, fixed ideas and preformulated strategies are of little value. Technique which may be effective one moment is virtually guaranteed not to work the next. In many instances, particularly when the fear of losing is in the back of one's mind, there is the danger that one may read strengths into the adversary's game that may in fact be nonexistent. The fencer may well find himself or herself fencing against a projection of personal imagination instead of the opponent, who is really there and who will happily take advantage of any misunderstanding. Conversely, having scored a touch or two, the fencer may read weaknesses into the opponent's game, assuming that victory is a foregone conclusion. Armed with this preconceived "victory" the fencer may underestimate the adversary's strength and ability to change. This syndrome is well known and is frequently the reason for a fencer's starting off strongly and finishing in defeat.

Psychological Vision

The fencer must develop a perceptual ability to observe clearly and sensitively the changing patterns of movement and intentions of his or her adversary. The fencer's vision must be free of rigid preconceptions that can easily bind him or her to the second-by-second changes which take place on the fencing ground. The experienced fencer assumes nothing and sees everything. The fencer must be sensitive to the sights, sounds, and tactile elements of fencing interaction, observing distance, movement, and tempo, which are the only reliable bases upon which the formulation of sound fencing habits can be made. Technique can only serve the fencer in a creative manner once the strictly mechanical elements of fencing have been transcended. Pure technical approaches to fencing are doomed to failure, for they inadvertently leave out the personality and mind of the individual.

Sparring sessions that are used for the purpose of refining one's game can lead to a gradual and healthy psychological awakening, which is the means by which fencing strength is gained. One's sparring partner is used as an educational tool, serving as a reality check to one's fencing development. A good sparring partner is always alert and ready to let one know where one's fencing weaknesses lie. It is strongly recommended that one fence a wide variety of fencers with each sparring session. The broader the variety of fencing experience one can gain, the faster one's game will mature.

FENCING FOCUS

The reader may speculate on how one can fence without focusing solely on winning and losing, especially when the object of the game is to defeat an adversary. I am not suggesting that one abandon the notion that winning is important, or that one should voluntarily lose for the sake of a fencing education. But it is always the best course to focus one's attention on *fencing well* rather than on defeating someone. Victory is only the by-product of excellent fencing, it is never the by-product of some neurotic need to defeat someone. Of the many first-rate champions I have been privileged to know, not one of them was concerned with a personal victory over another individual. However, they are all intrigued with the endlessly interesting *process* of fencing. The fencer who is compulsively focused on "victory" will never be a champion, for this type of individual finds it impossible to concentrate long enough for realistic practice. As has been suggested, there are no shortcuts to a strong game.

The successful fencer practices constantly. Every opportunity, from the sparring session to the tournament environment, becomes another learning experience for the fencer who wishes to improve.

TACTICAL ADVANTAGE

All speculation relating to tactics must be general. There are no standards by which one can analyze or itemize exactly what it takes to win against a strong fencer. Champions come in all sizes and shapes, employing many diverse approaches. In any given fencing match one is confronted with the most complex problem in sports, that of human nature. Unlike sports such as archery and bowling, where the target is stationary, fencing requires that one work against a moving target which is intelligent, trained, and able to defend itself. The fencer must score not only against his or her adversary's target, but also must assume the responsibility of defending his or her own. The nature of the relationship established, though simple, is as complex as human nature itself.

Tactical Premise

The basic premise of fencing rests in the concept that theoretically two perfect fencers cannot score against each other. For every attack there is a defense, and for every counterattack there exists a counterdefense. This implies that the only available means for the fencer to find scoring opportunities is through the discovery of imperfections in the opponent's defense. The purpose of fencing tactics is to create openings in the adversary's defense through which a scoring touch may be delivered while at the same time protecting one's own target. This assignment is not a simple matter, for one's adversary may be very skilled and will make every effort to do the same in return. It is essential that the fencer be familiar with basic strategic approaches if tactics are to be effective and realistic.

Tactical Comparisons

Every sport has its own unique nature, and fencing is not an exception. In making comparisons with the other individual combative skill sports, this premise is easily understood. For example, the ultimate goal in boxing is to immobilize the adversary's mental process. Here, the "knockout" punch is the completed achievement of the boxer's skill. This stands in direct contrast to wrestling, where one's skill is ultimately proven through the immobilization of the adversary's body. The martial art of Judo (the gentle way) finds success through deflection. Judo defense does not work to immobilize the adversary, but rather to deflect aggressive energy, allowing it to pass harmlessly by. Judo skill essentially redirects the opponent's energy or physical commitment.

Fencing strategy rests in its ability to *distract* the adversary's attention, throwing it off balance, which has the effect of triggering uncontrolled reflex responses and encouraging errors in tactical judgment. The effective strategist will control the adversary's intention, leading him or her into traps where a scoring touch can be delivered. The fencer attempts to score at the exact moment when defense is made impossible. Fencing is a purely mental relationship that expresses itself between two people through tactical arrangements in which each person tries to bring the adversary's perception, involuntary responses, and offensive energy under control. Advanced-level fencing avoids all body contact, and establishes its relationship through distance, timing, movement, and mental confrontation. Defensively, fencing has much in common with Judo. The fencer makes no attempt to immobilize the adversary's attack but rather, by use of the parry, redirects the offending blade, causing it to pass ineffectually by the target. The fencer places no importance on direct physical confrontation, and it is for this reason that one cannot identify a physical prototype in fencing. The following premises are presented as a convenient guide to basic fencing tactics:

1. As a *first* tactical intention the fencer should abandon physical force and purely physical confrontation as a basic means toward scoring.
2. Offensive scoring should be a by-product of attacks which basically prepare by distracting the opponent's mental and reflex responses through the use of feints, beats, etc.
3. Basic defensive scoring should be achieved as a by-product of the opponent's offensive energy, thus creating the time in which the riposte can be used to advantage.
4. All other methods of scoring such as stop thrusts and attacks into tempo are designed to take advantage of the adversary's lapses in attention and overt tactical and technical errors. The fencer must and should score in any manner available to him which does not create body contact. In the final analysis, if it works, use it.
5. Finally, whatever the circumstances, the fencer must remain centered in the essential reality of fencing, which is that of a predominantly *mental contest*. It is far more effective to *think one's way through the adversary's defense* than to resort to brute strength.

BOUTING STRATEGY

Once the command to "fence" is given, all theoretical considerations cease to be academic. The fencer must now put into practice the theories and techniques studied. The first task at hand is to ensure that

Fig. 10.2. Two fencers exploring and probing possibilities, searching for the exact moment when a scoring opportunity will reveal itself.

the adversary does not gain an immediate surprise advantage. The fencer begins the match by probing to draw out the opponent's intentions and potentials, alert to the possibility that the opponent may attack without warning at any time. Psychological vision and a sound defense are especially important during this initial phase of the bout, where the primary task is to gather information upon which to base continued strategy. The following list offers a general idea of the kinds of information one is looking for.

1. Is the opponent confident? Will intimidation work as a tactic?
2. Does the opponent stand ground, or is mobility a strong factor to his or her technique?
3. Does the opponent press forward, closing distance, or does he or she prefer to fence at long distance?
4. Is the opponent prone to attack? If so, how does the attack materialize? Are attacks direct or indirect? Will stop thrusts or parries serve the best interests of defense?
5. Does the opponent retreat out of distance when attacked? How far?
6. Is the opponent prone to parry or stop thrust?
7. Does the opponent respond to feints and beats?
8. Does the opponent consistently repeat the same parries and attacks?
9. Is the opponent prone to fleché, lunge, or pattinando?
10. Is the opponent prone to remise or redouble after completion of the offensive?

This would appear to be a sizable amount of information to gain in the course of a minute or two. However, with bouting experience, the fencer will be able to make these judgments and more, and in a very short time. Conversely, the fencer should make every attempt to conceal as much information as possible from the adversary, while supplying as much false information as possible, weakening the opponent's possiblities for a tactical advantage. It is of crucial importance that the fencer never allow the adversary knowledge of how he or she intends to score. The following list suggests practical tactics that may be used as a basic approach to creating a scoring advantage:

1. Keep your adversary guessing about distance. Alternately press forward and then pull away. This push-pull use of distance is most unnerving to all fencers. Keep moving, attempting to gain a sur-

prise element for the attack when the opportunity finally presents itself. The opponent is at an immediate disadvantage if it is impossible to pin one down to a specific place on the fencing ground. A moving target is difficult to score against. In frustration, the opponent may be motivated to attack at an inopportune moment, rendering his or her offensive effort less effective. When attacks fail, it always has a demoralizing effect on the fencer, especially if a riposte has been successful. As each attack fails, the adversary will feel the options narrowing, creating psychological pressure which can lead to continued frustration and mistakes.

2. Keep the opponent busy with reconnaissance actions, such as beats to the blade and changes in one's guard position. Moving the guard alternately from sixte to octave and vice versa is most effective. Present the blade and then withdraw it. When the adversary expects an attack, withhold it. When the adversary expects action, stay back and remain still. When things settle down, move. Keep the adversary guessing. *Never show what you want.*

3. When the opponent demonstrates specific strengths, prevent them from materializing further. For example, if the adversary possesses a strong defensive game, don't attack. Conversely, if the adversary has a powerful offense, don't allow it to get started. This is best done by exerting one's own offensive pressure and forcing the opponent into a defensive game. Under all circumstances, insist that the adversary fence against *your* strongest game.

4. Maintain control of the fencing tempo. Keep the tempo irregular with sudden changes in movement which alternate from fast to slow and vice versa. Set up rhythmic patterns and break them. Start-stop, push-pull, attack!

5. Effective defense should be varied, alternating between circular, horizontal, and vertical parry systems. This creates a context in which it becomes most difficult for the opponent to formulate effective offensive strategy.

6. Avoid premature parries. It is unwise to parry unless the attacking blade is at least within six inches of the target. Ignore the opponent's beats, feints, and general preparation. Parry only the "real thing" which is *always* the final thrust of any offensive preparation. This delayed response will draw the opponent to the conclusion of the lunge, a position where all offensive energy has been expended, thus setting the stage for a smashing riposte which is delivered exactly at the moment when the attacker is least able to

Figure 10.3.

defend. The one exception to this rule occurs when the attacker's feints are slow, in which case one may parry early, parrying the feint itself. While this strategy should be used rarely and with caution, it always creates a shocking surprise, leaving the attacker incapable of a defensive counter-reaction for protection from the riposte.

7. Never overuse successful tactics. Once a weakness is discovered in the adversary's defense and a scoring touch has been made, don't repeat the scoring tactic immediately. Play around, distracting the opponent's attention from it, and then return to score again. Save your effective scoring technique for the moment when it can be delivered as a total surprise. All fencers are vulnerable to this tactical procedure when it is used properly. Within the context of bouting, the opponent's memory can be manipulated. The fencer who takes advantage of opportunities based on this premise will earn many extra points, even though his or her technique may be limited.

8. Alternate defense with stop thrusts. Keep the adversary guessing as to whether parries or stopping action will be your defense. The experienced fencer encourages his or her opponent to perform complex preparation in an attempt to create circumstances wherein stop thrusts can be used to advantage. Conversely, the opponent who has been scored against with a stop thrust will be inclined to attack directly on the next offensive, in which case the parry and riposte should be waiting.

9. Fight hard for every touch, regardless of the score. If the score is three or four to zero against one's adversary, one must still fight for the last touch or touches, as hard as for the first. *Never* slack off in the face of near success. Don't allow the opponent an opportunity to make a comeback, which frequently happens. Changing one's game at the moment of near-victory is an all-too-common error with which every fencer can identify. This syndrome has caused defeat for many excellent competitors.

10. If one is behind on the score sheet, renewed efforts must be made. The fencer must not lose heart under these disconcerting circumstances. Remember, the adversary runs a very real danger of overconfidence when in the lead and may well change tactics as victory is assumed. Also it must be observed that when one is winning, the last touch of the bout is always more difficult to

achieve than the first one. The fencer cannot escape the importance of the last touch, and if there exists a tendency to get nervous or distracted it will reveal itself at this crucial moment. Catching up is not impossible or necessarily difficult for one who manages to maintain his or her "cool".

11. Finally, fencers must *never* allow themselves the luxury of losing their tempers. Regardless of provocation, a loss of temper will *always* weaken one's game. Getting mad not only wastes valuable energy but serves as the ultimate distraction to one's tactical sense. Loss of temper is always the sign of a real loser, for it is impossible to meet the demands of fencing interaction when in a high-pitched emotional state. There are no champions with temper problems.

NERVOUS ENERGY

Every fencer to some degree will exhibit nervous habits which can be magnified or soothed by a skilled fencing tactician. It becomes the task of every fencer to recognize and control the nervous energy of the opponent. This is perhaps the single most important means the fencer has available with which to dominate the fencing ground. For example, if one's opponent is highly excitable, it may be a sound tactical judgment to calm him or her down in preparation for an attack. This sets the stage for a beat or feint which will cause an uncontrolled release of pent-up energy and may present an opening through which an attack can be delivered. This is similiar to the reaction one could imagine if someone were to stand behind a door in a dark room and jump out unexpectedly to yell "BOO!" at an unsuspecting visitor. On the other hand, the fencer may *create* nervous excitement in an effort to disrupt a particularly relaxed and confident opponent. This is easily accomplished by introducing rapid and erratic footwork and blade play into the bout, disrupting the adversary's concentration and causing tension in his or her technique.

BODY LANGUAGE AND TIMING

It is important to understand that the instant the fencing mask is dropped over one's face and the command to fence is given, one's total attention becomes automatically fixed on the adversary. The adversary's movements and intentions become magnified. The fencer will record and respond intensely to the opponent's every gesture. The fencer who is aware of this unique relationship will employ *body language* as an integral aspect of strategy.

If the speed of one's movements is increased or slowed down, the adversary will most likely follow suit. When the fencer advances, the opponent will, as a reflex response, be inclined to retreat and vice versa. When one becomes conscious of the nearly automatic nature of this relationship, it becomes the single most effective tool with which to control and ultimately defeat one's adversary. Consciousness of this tactical possibility also frees one from being victimized by it. The reason this approach is effective is that one's adversary may not realize what is happening, at least not until it is too late. With the use of body language one's adversary may be led into some interesting traps. For example, the fencer may retreat, anticipating that the opponent will advance. Then, at the instant of the advance, the ideal time in which to attack has been created, catching the opponent during the forward step when a retreat cannot be used as a defense. This strategy is the heart and core of good timing, which is defined as *the most opportune moment* in which to execute a fencing action. Effective timing always creates the element of surprise.

Awareness of nervous disposition coupled with an understanding that the adversary is hypersensitive to movement can open up entire fields of tactical speculation. It is this knowledge that gives technique life. The elements of tempo, timing, and distance become the central reality of fencing. Technique serves as a medium through which this reality can be expressed. Technique is formed by this reality, which, for lack of a better word, we call fencing.

SHORT AND TALL FENCERS

The short fencer with a limited reach has a natural advantage when fencing at close distance. Here the longer reach of the tall fencer becomes a distinct disadvantage. The short fencer must contrive a pattern of offensive moves to work inside the reach of the taller fencer before delivering the final thrust of the attack. Timing, distance, and speed are of special importance in this effort, and stop thrusts present a particular danger. The taller fencer normally depends on a long reach as a means to scoring and is inclined to overuse stopping action. This habit is frequently predictable, making the task of the shorter fencer less difficult. The shorter fencer should employ second intention tactics, drawing out his or her opponent's reach, taking command of the blade with a parry or beat, and moving in rapidly for the scoring thrust. Once inside, and in the event the attack misses or is parried, close distance should be maintained as an advantage for parries, ripostes, remises, and possible infighting. The necessity for accelerated movement suggests that the pattinando and ballestra are the surest means to this end.

The taller fencer must be prepared to retreat and parry when attacks and stopping actions fail. Reach and balance must not be overextended during offensive movements where distance is easily closed to the short fencer's advantage.

THE LEFT-HANDED FENCER

If there is a natural advantage in fencing, it most certainly belongs to the left-handed fencer. This advantage is one of circumstances, created because most fencers, being right-handed, find less opportunity to practice against lefties. Conversely, the lefty finds ample practice opportunities against right-handed fencers. However, like the tall fencer who is inclined to develop dependence on a long reach, the lefty is inclined to habits which work as a disadvantage when confronted with a knowledgeable adversary.

The left-handed fencer will usually have a strong quarte parry and riposte, and will overuse it because of its genuine effectiveness. This overuse creates a weak sixte and octave line, of which one should take all possible advantage. The lefty can usually be counted on to overreact to feints and beats which prepare in the quarte line. When failing to find the blade in quarte, the lefty will frequently follow through to second (octave) parry, where, if the blade is still not found, the defense continues around, up, and back to the quarte position. This secondary overreaction to second suggests that feints to the second or low outside line are excellent strategy.

The following suggestions work well as general tactical principles when fencing the lefty. It must also be noted that the same material works to excellent advantage when used by the left-handed fencer against the right-handed fencer.

Offense

Avoid attacks which are designed to score to the lefty's quarte line. One may prepare attacks with feints, beats, etc. in all lines, but the final thrust of the attack is best delivered to the left-hander's sixte or octave lines. In effect, *attacks scoring to the outside high and low lines have an excellent chance of scoring.* If the lefty catches the attacking blade in the quarte parry, the riposte will be very strong and difficult to parry. Attacks which are specially designed for use against the left-handed fencer are:

a) Feints or beats addressed to the quarte line, disengaging to the outside high or low lines of sixte and octave.
b) Feints and beats addressing themselves to the sixte line followed through with a one, two disengage, returning to score in the sixte outside high line or octave outside low line.
c) Feints to the octave line, disengaging up and around the outside of the defending parry to score to the sixte outside high line.
d) Beat in sixte, coupé over to quarte, disengage to score to the octave or outside low line. This attack is best performed with the ballestra or pattinando.
e) Take the blade in sixte, enveloping the blade to score to the octave outside low line. Best performed with pattinando or ballestra.

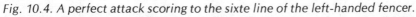

Fig. 10.4. A perfect attack scoring to the sixte line of the left-handed fencer.

Defense

1. The lefty will invariably attack to the defender's octave outside low line or the quarte inside high line, making these lines of defense foremost. The combination parries of circular sixte and quarte, or circular sixte and octave are recommended defenses. The circular sixte parry keeps the high outside line tight in the event of feint or beat preparation to the sixte line, and still provides for a follow-through to quarte or octave, where one can expect to be attacked. This defense is also strongly recommended to the left-handed fencer, whose sixte line, as suggested, always needs extra attention.

2. Ripostes are best delivered to the lefty's octave outside low line, scoring anywhere to the back. Also, ripostes to the sixte line and shoulder work well. Ripostes which feint to quarte are excellent against those who can be counted on not to remise.

3. Stop thrusts to the sixte line are most effective. The lefty loves to prepare attacks with beats or takes into the right-hander's sixte. This opens the lefty's sixte line during preparation, making it vulnerable to stopping action

Fig. 10.5. The fencer to the left attempts a riposte to the left-handed fencer's octave line.

Fig. 10.6. The left-handed fencer scores with a counter action to the opponent's octave line.

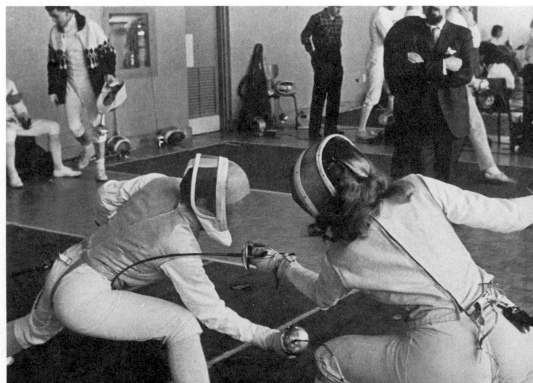

CHAPTER 11

JUDGING AND DIRECTING STANDARD FOIL

STANDARD FOIL

While all official championship fencing is performed electrically, there are always occasions in which one may gain tournament experience with the standard foil. Usually these are informal practice tournaments which are held in one's club or school, but one may still find A.F.L.A. and collegiate novice meets which do not require electrical equipment. Standard foil tournaments are most beneficial, offering a formal setting to the fencer in which new techniques and approaches may be tested.

The standard foil tournament also offers the fencer valuable first-hand experience in judging and directing. All fencers should be encouraged to gain judging and directing experience as a means to strengthening their power of observation and conceptions of a valid touch and right-of-way. Judging and directing can be learned only within the context of the tournament environment, where the fencer has an opportunity to actually make the difficult decisions concerning touches and right-of-way.

The Fencing Strip [Piste]

The regulation fencing strip or field of play measures from 1.8 to 2.0 meters wide and extends 14 meters in length. The strip may be shorter if space is not available, but never less than 10 meters. A 1½- to 2-meter run-off space must be provided on each end of the strip. The surface can be wood, linoleum, cork, rubber, etc., and it must be smooth and free of hazards which can cause slipping or tripping. The strip must be marked to indicate the center, the on-guard line, the warning lines, and the rear limit lines. (See Fig. 11.1.)

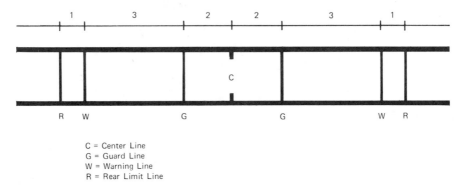

C = Center Line
G = Guard Line
W = Warning Line
R = Rear Limit Line

Fig. 11.1. Regulation fencing piste in meters.

The Guard Lines

The fencer salutes his or her opponent and assumes the guard position from behind the guard line. They then wait for the command to fence from the director of the bout. Once fencing has started, the fencer is free to carry out action on any part of the ground as long as both feet are on the strip.

The Warning Line

Should the fencer be driven back to his or her own end of the strip, so that one foot touches the warning line, the director must call *halt*, stopping the action. The director then warns the fencer that the rear limit line is one meter away. After receiving this warning, if the fencer regains ground, reaching the guard line with one foot, the warning is nullified. In the event that one is driven back to the rear limit line a second time before a valid touch has been scored, an additional warning must be granted, and so on.

The Rear Limit Line

After receiving a warning and if one does not regain the guard line, an automatic touch will be awarded against the fencer who is driven over the rear limit line with both feet.

When either fencer has been scored against three times, the opponents shake hands and exchange sides of the strip. This exchange is
required so that each fencer may share a possible visual advantage that
may be gained on one side of the strip or the other. Also, this trading of
positions on the strip enables each fencer to equally share judges, who
are stationed on each end of the ground and who do not change sides as
do the fencers.

An exception to this rule occurs when right- and left-handed fencers compete against each other. Because of their physical circumstances, the right- and left-handed fencers must always fence with their
sword arms to the same side of the strip. In this case, the director always
positions himself to the fencers' open or front side to gain better visual
advantage. At midpoint in the bout, when one of the fencers has been
scored against three times, the *judges* change sides. In this way the
open side of the fencing remains facing the director.

JUDGING

There are four judges, who are assigned in pairs and are stationed slightly behind and off the strip near each fencer. (See Figs. 11.2 and 11.3.)
Each pair of judges will observe the fencer on the end of the ground opposite from themselves. The judges to the right observe the fencer to
the left, while the judges to the left observe the fencer to the right. In
effect, two judges watch one fencer. This arrangement creates visual
efficiency, providing each set of judges with a maximum opportunity to
observe the validity of any given touch. The judges are assigned the

Fig. 11.2. Directing and judging.

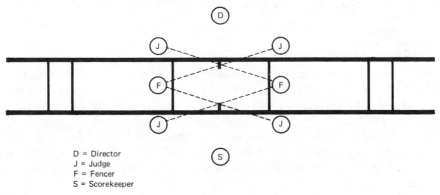

D = Director
J = Judge
F = Fencer
S = Scorekeeper

specific tasks of determining by observation when a fencer has been scored against. As the fencers move from one end of the strip to the other, the judges move with them, maintaining the same physical relationship to the activity of the bout.

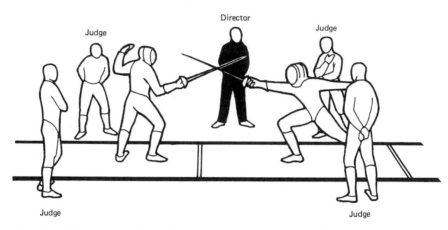

Fig. 11.3. Directing and judging.

The Judges' Vote

Each judge has one vote. Upon seeing a touch scored, the judge raises his or her hand to signal the director of the bout that a touch has been scored. The director will then call "halt," stopping the action, and poll each judge for an opinion. The judges may express opinions relative to any given fencing action with a "yes," "no," or "abstention."

VOTING CRITERIA

1. The judge may indicate a *yes vote* if a touch has been scored either on or off the valid target. The judge may indicate yes, a valid touch has been scored; or yes, the touch scored, but off target. The duration of a touch may be for only a split-second to be valid. However, the judge must ensure that valid hits are called only when the point of the weapon has securely scored against the target with enough penetrating power to bend the foil blade. Attacks which slap or

miss the target must not be considered as either *fair* or *off-target* hits. Beginners frequently call anything which lands to the off target an off-target hit. The beginner must be mindful that *all* hits must be with the point.

2. The judge may indicate a *no vote* only if the attack is *clearly seen* to have missed the valid or nonvalid targets.

3. The judge may *abstain* if the action is not clear, or when it may be doubtful about what has happened. A good judge will abstain frequently rather than force judgments of which he or she is not sure.

THE DIRECTOR

The director has the responsibility for the conduct of the bout. The director must ensure that the fencing is done fairly and without danger to the contestants. The director starts and stops all action and keeps the scorekeeper informed on all decisions made by the jury. In addition, the director may vote on the materiality of touches. Where the judges have one vote, the director has a vote and one-half and may overrule an individual judge. However, when two judges on one side vote together their two votes overrule the director.

Directing Right-of-Way

In addition to other responsibilities, the director must also determine fencing right-of-way in the event that both fencers score simultaneously. The director is constantly watchful for the beginning of each fencing phrase. The director must know which fencer establishes the attack and what subsequent actions lead to a scoring touch which ends the phrase. When polling the judges, the director must reconstruct the fencing phrase so that each judge will know which part of the action is being voted on. For example: the fencer to the director's right makes an attack; the fencer to the left makes a parry riposte, which the fencer on the right counter-parries, scoring with a counter-riposte. The judges' hands are raised as the director halts the action. The director must now poll the judges on every movement of the phrase, thus establishing for the judges and the fencers alike what has taken place. Upon reconstructing the phrase, the director will ask the judges to the right if the original attack scored. Upon receiving two no votes, the judges to the left are asked if the riposte arrived. Upon receiving two no votes, the judges to the right, who originally raised their hands, are asked if the counter-riposte landed. Both judges vote yes, and the touch is awarded against the fencer on the left.

Naturally, every phrase will not receive unanimous votes on all actions. All touches which have established a right-of-way priority and which also have received a voting majority will be awarded the point. If the judges and the director all abstain on a part of the phrase, the entire phrase is thrown out. If the director abstains and the judges disagree, voting yes and no, the action is thrown out. If the director cannot reconstruct the phrase which enables right-of-way to be determined, when all judges vote yes, the action is thrown out.

Figure 11.4.

FENCING FOR THE JURY

It is important when fencing standard foil that the fencer make all actions as visually clear as possible. This is where form is so important. The fencer must keep foremost in mind that the touch is defined as *one seen by the jury* and not necessarily as one that arrives. It is the fencer's responsibility to prove to the jury that a touch has been established. The fencer who concentrates on good form, clear action, and well-delivered touches which score to visually exposed areas of the target increases the chances for a victory. Because of the necessity to prove one's skill to the jury, the fencer not only must score, but must score *well* if a true advantage is to be created. Because of this, it is my opinion that standard foil fencing is the best possible foundation for every fencer.

Figure 12.1

CHAPTER 12

MODERN ELECTRIC FOIL FENCING

The electric foil has permanently changed our concept of fencing. It has effected a modernization of fencing technique which has been subtle but gradual and has brought forth several implications for the modern fencer. The implications are not difficult to understand if the fundamental reason for change is seen in its proper context. The context is the traditional standard game, while the reason for change is the introduction of the electrical scoring device.

The standard foil is now relegated in use to informal recreation fencing, where it is regarded as a practice weapon with which one may learn fencing or prepare for the ultimate fencing experience, which is now found only through the electric weapon. One may still find those who see this change as a negative departure from the tried and true practices of traditional classic fencing, who maintain that the electrical game encourages substandard methodology when compared with traditional foil practices. In answer, one can only point to the performances of top-level fencers, where excellence is still reflected in balance, conditioning, and lucid tactics, which have become more important to good fencing than ever before.

As one observes modern fencing tactics emerging from the context of electrical foil, it is most interesting to note that the basic techniques of fencing have changed very slightly. The modern fencer's parries and

Figure 12.2

Figure 12.3

Figure 12.4

Figure 12.5

attacks remain essentially the same. The issues of balance, timing, tempo, distance, tactical advantage, and physical conditioning now reflect the true anatomy of electric foil competitive strength. The modern fencer must be familiair with the potentials inherent in the electrical game if success is to be found in today's long, hard-fought competitions.

CONDITIONING

The modern game, because of its emphasis on greater speed, where touches can be scored faster than visual perception, demands that the fencer train as an athlete. With older fencing styles, the primary defensive emphasis centered on the fencer's ability to parry. The parry was the steel wall through which the attack was refused penetration. Footwork and mobility were given secondary consideration in defense. The modern fencer places equal emphasis on mobility and parries as defensive means. A strong retreat accompanying defensive hand action is common. Today's fencer must parry attacks which are faster than ever before and are frequently intended for traditionally obscure areas of the target. This relatively contemporary emphasis on mobility as a defensive means places additional physical demands not only on the defender, but also on the attacker, who is forced to travel farther and faster for each scoring touch. With today's extended fencing distance one cannot depend on simple lunging action for scoring effectiveness. The pattinando, ballestra, and fleché have become essential ingredients to offensive scoring ability.

The modern fencing athlete must supplement his or her normal training program with additional strenuous exercise such as running and calisthenics, which are designed to increase endurance, flexibility, and strength. A balanced running program consisting of jogging and wind-sprints becomes the fencer's surest means to both stamina and a well-developed cardio-respiratory system. Stretching exercises of all kinds are especially helpful in keeping the muscles flexible and supple. The fencer's legs need special conditioning, for they carry the burden of all offensive action. The serious fencer must conscientiously lunge daily if his or her legs are to effectively meet the challenges of today's tournament fencing, where one will be required to perform hundreds of attacks in a single afternoon's competition. Fifty well-executed lunges per day, in addition to the normal lunging performed during regular practice sessions, will make a world of difference to performance.

Figs. 12.6 through 12.22. The following sequence of stretching exercises is recommended to every fencer. Exercises of this nature are especially designed as a means to warming up in preparation for fencing, thus preventing strained or pulled muscles. Fifteen to twenty minutes of this preparation before each class session or tournament will ensure that one is ready to meet the physical demands made by fencing.

While one must be mindful that fencing implies a mental confrontation, it should be recognized that excellent physical conditioning is a prerequisite to successful tournament results.

TIMING

Because of the increasing emphasis on speed, the modern fencer must resort to more simplified movement. There is little time for complex action, and this factor, in turn, places a premium on timing. The competitor who sacrifices speed for the complex action will invariably discover that his or her time has been usurped by a simple, fast, and well-planned direct action. The modern attack is prone to be done *into tempo* or *into preparation*. This is the rule in today's fencing, whereas it was the exception in the older standard foil game.

TEMPO

Because of the emphasis on speed and split-second timing, the general tempo of modern fencing is shorter. Also, the modern context forces the fencer to fence at least one full tempo ahead of any given action. One must always be prepared to accept an attack into preparation which requires a second intention game at all times. The fencers who cannot play this mentally and physically exhausting game reduce their chances to win.

DISTANCE

Again, because of attacks which are delivered into preparation, the modern fencer must maintain absolute control of distance. The modern game makes it dangerous and extremely difficult to defend against an attack that is developed within lunging distance. The modern fencer will not cooperate in offering his or her fencing measure. He or she is a specialist at manipulating distance and will not give the adversary a hint relating to how far an attack must travel to score.

REFINING ONE'S GAME

Since conditioning, timing, tempo, and distance are the more overt characteristics of the modern game, an accompanying refinement in technique is also observable. The modern fencer must lunge, parry, and generally move better than ever before. At its accelerated speed, modern fencing places extra emphasis on balance, mechanical control, and a thorough knowledge of right-of-way. Technique in general is undergoing a refinement that was unnecessary in the standard game. Parries are designed to be lighter, faster, and most importantly clear. The modern fencer is no longer concerned with "blocking" the attack, but instead parries only enough to gain right-of-way for the riposte. Footwork is lighter and always on the move, never allowing the weight to settle. The attack cannot afford to be slow or faulty in developing and must be delivered in one tempo. Complicated action has given way to the faster, more critically timed action. There is no longer a "conversation of the blades" in the old sense.

The modern electrical game requires a higher degree of technical control than before. The electrical foil is heavier and inclined to whip during fast action. Action on the blade must be executed with a minimum of blade movement, otherwise control is easily lost. Actions which depend on complicated blade movement are used infrequently.

THE TARGET

The target area in the modern electrical game offers different possibilities than with the standard game. Where attacks to the low line and back were rarely used in the standard game, they are now used extensively in the electrical game. Often, touches made in low line or to the back side with the standard foil were not seen by officials, so the fencer based most of his or her strategy on high-line touches to the front of the target. The electric foil allows the attack to be delivered with complete confidence to all areas of the target. The electric game offers attacks and ripostes to visually obscure areas of the target, and the implications to general strategy are far-reaching. Attacks to the underarm (octave) and ripostes to the back are now essential considerations to the modern electric game. (See Figs. 12.23 and 12.24.) In effect, the modern fencer protects twice as much target as the person fencing standard foil. Modern defense systems and tactics are designed with this very real consideration in mind. The standard foil fencer of yesterday's competition would be amazed to discover attacks scoring which were impossible or at best a gamble in the standard visually judged bout.

Fig. 12.23. Scoring from the top down and bottom up.

Fig. 12.24. Any port in a storm.

INFIGHTING

The electrical foil is responsible for the increased use of infighting techniques. The director of the standard foil bout will normally discontinue action when infighting develops, because hits scored under such circumstances are virtually impossible to see. With the electrical scoring device, which records every hit regardless of speed, it is no longer necessary to stop the fencing action just because the fencing phrase becomes visually confused or disorderly. The modern fencer must be prepared to continue fighting even though the fencing phrase has been lost. It is only the poorly trained fencer who will *intentionally* instigate infighting as a basic means of scoring. However, one must be prepared to infight should it become unavoidable as a defense or means to scoring. The skilled fencer will avoid infighting whenever possible. Infighting is, at best, a last resort, for technique works to minimum advantage in this context, allowing the opponent increased chances for an accidental touch.

Infighting occurs at close distance where one is unable to parry and can find no available means to sustain the normal exchanges of the fencing phrase. This may result when two fencers attack simultaneously, or when one fencer recovers forward from an ineffectual

Fig. 12.25. Infighting. Both fencers lunge, unable to make a scoring touch.

Fig. 12.26. They recover forward, closing distance, where the fencing phrase cannot be maintained or reestablished.

Fig. 12.27. As the distance closes, both fencers pivot while the fencer to the left scores brilliantly to the back of the opponent.

attack into close proximity with a defender who refuses to retreat. At this moment both fencers are forced, through circumstances which place them within inches of each other, to hit as fast as possible before the other can respond. What usually takes place is a rapid series of remises and jabs which continue until one fencer or the other sustains a scoring touch. Surprisingly enough, there are methods by which one can increase the probability of scoring when confronted with a fencer who insists upon infighting strategy.

1. Avoid infighting at all costs by controlling distance. It takes two to infight, and the aware fencer should manage broad distance, preventing the infighter from creating his or her assumed infighting advantage. The infighter is usually helpless when confronted with an adversary who will not let it happen.

2. If infighting cannot be avoided, close the distance as tightly as possible by pivoting forward and leading with the rear shoulder. This will place the target deep inside the opponent's defense where it becomes difficult for his or her point to be withdrawn far enough to create a forward thrust which will have target upon which to score. When closing distance in this way, one's own sword arm is

Fig. 12.28. Infighting. Note that fencer to the left has gained the scoring advantage by closing distance with the left shoulder forward.

free to deliver a rapid series of thrusts directly into the opponent's inside line. (See Fig. 12.28.) If for any reason one cannot score to the inside line, one may pivot forward from the initial close infighting stance, thus turning one's back to the opponent while reaching up and over one's own sword arm shoulder to score down to whatever target the blade is able to find. (See Fig. 12.29.)

Fig. 12.29. Infighting.

3. Whatever the infighting circumstances, don't stop fighting until the director calls halt. Many fencers will stop action, thinking they have scored or been scored against, when in fact a touch has not been registered. This is the surest way to receive a touch when fencing an opponent who continues fighting.

Fig. 12.30. Electrical equipment. Note the metallic vest and the electrical foil which is connected to a body cord emerging from inside the fencer's sleeve.

EQUIPMENT

The transition from standard foil to electrical fencing requires only three special items of fencing equipment: the electric foil, the foil body cord, and the metallic vest. (See Fig. 12.30.)

Electric foils are available with all models of grips. The French grip is recommended, but because the electric weapon is slightly heavier than the standard foil, an orthopedic grip may offer advantages to fencers with small hands. In addition to the stiffer blade of the electric foil, its distinguishing features include a specialized tip and a body cord connector located inside the guard.

The electric tip includes the button, the button housing or barrel, and the button spring, which is found inside the housing. At the base of the housing, note the cup, which is the termination of a circuit wire and runs the length of the foil blade, connecting it to the body cord connector. The button spring exerts 500+ grams of pressure against the button, which must be depressed to complete the circuit if a valid touch is to be recorded on the scoring machine. (See Fig. 12.31.) This assemblage should be taken apart occasionally for cleaning and for adjustments or replacements of the spring, which may weaken in time. Reasonable maintenance will always ensure a dependable working foil.

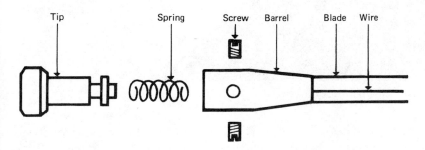

Fig. 12.31. The electric-foil tip.

The electric blade is insulated from the tip of the button housing back to no less than fifteen centimeters of the blade. The insulation tape prevents touches from grounding out against the opponent's target during what otherwise would be a scoring touch. In effect, if the bare metal of the blade touches the opponent's metallic vest simultaneously with a scoring touch, the circuitry will be grounded and the scoring touch will not be recorded. The fencer should make certain that the foil insulation does not wear off, especially around the button housing, where grounding contact is most easily made. It is good policy to check the condition of the insulation tape after each bout.

The pommel of the electric foil must also be insulated. If one's foil pommel touches one's own target during the time the adversary scores, the touch will not be recorded because of grounding.

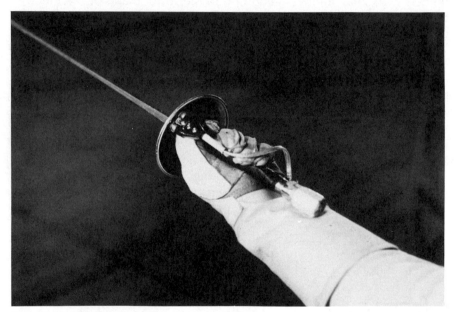

Fig. 12.32. The guard socket.

The body cord connection is located inside the foil guard. The fencer must be sure that the foil handle is on tightly to prevent this essential item from malfunctioning. A loose handle can sever the delicate wires connecting the body cord connector to the circuitry of the blade. This is the most common cause of foil malfunction and can be prevented with the slightest amount of care. Both before and after using one's foil, one should check to see that all aspects of its mechanics are in sound working order. This not only guarantees faithful service but greatly extends the life of the weapon. In fencing there is always one fencer who experiences continued problems with equipment. We all know why.

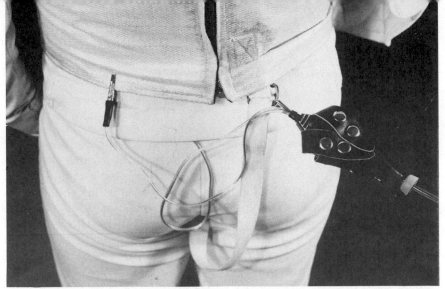

Fig. 12.33. *The body cord emerges from under the fencer's jacket where it connects to the reel cable. Note the small clip to the left which connects the electric vest to the circuitry.*

The Body Cord

The body cord runs from the connector up the inside of the fencer's sleeve, over the shoulder, and down the back to emerge from under the jacket, where it is connected to the scoring machine cable. (See Fig. 12.33.) This spring-operated cable releases and rewinds from a reel as the fencer moves forward and backward on the fencing ground. (See Fig. 12.34.) The tension created by the reel cable does not restrict or inhibit movements by the fencer, but allows complete freedom of movement while fencing. The reel is in turn connected to the scoring machine where every hit is recorded.

Fig. 12.34. *The cable reel. Note the cable to the right which completes the circuitry to the scoring machine.*

The Metallic Vest

The metallic vest covers and defines the valid scoring surface of the fencing target and is connected to the circuitry of the scoring machine. (See Fig. 12.35.) Touches scoring *on the vest* complete a circuit which activates a colored light and buzzer indicating a valid touch. Hits scoring *off target* travel through an alternate circuit, activating a white light and buzzer indicating a foul or off-target touch. This is a fool-proof system and the fencer is guaranteed that every valid and invalid touch will be recorded regardless of the speed with which it arrives or the duration of penetration.

Fig. 12.35. The scoring machine.

DIRECTING ELECTRIC FOIL

The Strip

The electric foil strip is covered with a copper screen which is grounded to prevent floor touches, which may otherwise be confused with off-target hits to one or the other of the competitors. Markings indicating the guard lines, warning lines, and the rear limit of the strip of electric foil are identical to those of the standard foil strip. In the event that a copper strip is unavailable, a floor judge must be assigned for each bout to distinguish between hits against the fencer and hits to the floor.

The Director

The electric foil director positions himself or herself so that the scoring machine and the fencing action can be seen simultaneously. As the fencers move back and forth on the strip the director moves with them, so that both the fencers and the machine are in one continuous line of vision. (See Fig. 12.36.) While the scoring machine replaces the traditional four judges of the standard foil jury, it does not replace the director, who must still determine which fencer possesses right-of-way in the event double touches are registered.

Fig. 12.36. Directing electric foil.

The Scoring Machine

As can be seen in Fig. 12.35, the scoring machine displays four lights across its top. The two lights to the right indicate touches scored *against* the valid or nonvalid target of the fencer to the right, while the lights to the left indicate touches *against* the fencer to the left. Each fencer has a colored light and a white light. The colored light on the right is red, while the light on the left is green. When a fencer's colored light is activated, it indicates a valid touch has been scored against that direction. When the white light is activated, an invalid touch to the off target has been scored. If both the colored and white lights on one side are on, the machine indicates that the fencer was scored off target before the valid touch was made. The machine will not record off-target hits against a fencer who has first received a valid touch. In an instance where all of the lights on the machine are activated, the director knows that both fencers were first scored against on the invalid target, followed by hits on the valid target.

Directing

The circuitry of the scoring machine is constructed so as to be consistent with considerations of right-of-way. Frequently, two colored lights or two colored lights and a white light will activate together, requiring the director to analyze and determine which fencer may have possessed an advantage of right-of-way. The following are typical examples of the kind of decisions the director must make to determine the priority of touches in a given bouting situation.

1. Fencer A attacks. Fencer B parries, scoring with a direct riposte, while fencer A remises, scoring to the valid target. Two colored lights are activated. The director determines that, while both fencers were scored upon, fencer A has the touch awarded against him or her because a remise cannot gain time against a direct riposte.

2. Fencer A attacks. Fencer B parries and ripostes simultaneously with fencer A's remise. Fencer A's white light and fencer B's red light are activated. The director awards no touch because fencer B's riposte, which gained right-of-way, scored off target, invalidating fencer B's remise.

3. Fencer A attacks. Fencer B parries and ripostes with a disengage against a direct remise by fencer A. Both colored lights are activated. The director must award the touch against fencer B, who invalidated right-of-way by performing a two-tempo riposte against a direct remise.

4. Fencer A attacks. Fencer B parries and misses on a direct riposte. Fencer A immediately remises. Fencer B remises. Two colored lights are activated. The director awards the touch against fencer B, who invalidated the riposte by missing, in which instance the right-of-way passes back to fencer A's remise.

5. Fencer A attacks direct. Fencer B stop thrusts. Fencer A's colored light and fencer B's white light are activated. The director awards no touch because the right-of-way was carried with the attack. The off-target touch does not count as a score, of course.

6. Fencers A and B attack simultaneously. Lights on both sides are activated. The director awards no touch because both fencers extended together, invalidating each other's right-of-way.

CHAPTER 13

THE TOURNAMENT AND TOURNAMENT STRATEGY

Tournament fencing offers to the competitor the richest experience available in fencing. Here one may fence against a wide variety of fencing styles which will test one's technique in a way that recreational practice cannot hope to do. After a day of tournament fencing, regardless of whether one has won or lost, the fencer will have gained insights that will last as material for practice for weeks to come. The tournament season lasts from October to June, which allows the participant ample opportunity for tournament exposure on any skill level desired. The fencing tournament attracts people from all walks of life, and offers them associations that frequently last a lifetime. Fencing becomes, in a very real sense, a vehicle for people to express their common interest in a sport they find fascinating.

Tournament fencing is available on both the collegiate and non-collegiate levels. Collegiate fencing is normally conducted through duel meets or round robin tournaments where several schools meet at one time. This affords an excellent learning environment where new ideas and techniques are gained. The student who qualifies for this activity will enjoy visiting other schools where competition is always managed under enjoyable sporting conditions.

For those not fencing collegiately, the Amateur Fencer's League of America offers a full schedule of competitive events through its local divisions which are open to anyone interested in fencing. A.F.L.A. tournaments range from novice meets to championship events. Top fencers from the local or divisional level qualify to compete in the National Championships, which alternate each year between the east and west coasts.

The A.F.L.A. is structured along divisional and sectional lines throughout the United States. For example, California belongs to the Pacific Coast Section and is divided into the Northern and Southern California Divisions. Both of these divisions send qualifiers to the Pacific Coast Sectional Championships and eventually to the United States National Championships. The step from the divisional level of competition to the National Championships, where Olympic points may be earned, is very short and uncluttered by political considerations. To qualify for the National Championships, one need only place among the top fencers on a divisional level through a single qualifying event which is usually held in May of each year.

CLASSIFICATION

Divisional tournaments are classified according to general performance and include unclassified, Class C, Class B, and Class A competitions. One may always fence above one's class level, but never below it. The following list describes each classification included in A.F.L.A. competition:

1. Unclassified Competition

All fencers who have never earned a classification are eligible to fence in this event. The winner of an official unclassified tournament earns the rank of a Class C competitor. To be official, the unclassified tournament must include a minimum of eighteen entries.

2. Class C Competition

This tournament is open to Class C as well as to unclassified fencers. The first place winner of a Class C event earns a Class C ranking. An official Class C competition must include a minimum of twelve contestants, which leads to a final round of six fencers. Two of the six finalists must already be classified as C fencers. In the event a Class C fencer wins a Class C tournament he or she remains Class C.

3. Class B Competition

Entries may include unclassified, Class C, and Class B fencers. The winner of a Class B tournament earns a Class B ranking. The competition must consist of at least two rounds, with the final round including not less than six fencers, two of whom must be Class B and two Class C or higher. The Class B competition must include a minimum of fifteen entries.

4. Class A Competition

This tournament is open to all fencing classifications. The winner of a Class A event earns a Class A ranking. The competition must include a minimum of fifteen contestants, at least six of whom are ranked C or higher. The final round must include six fencers, two of whom are classified as A and two as B or higher.

Classified tournaments are always held as individual events. A large tournament will include from twenty to thirty contestants. The tournament is structured according to elimination rounds which are fenced on a round-robin basis. Contestants are "seeded" according to relative strength, to ensure that each preliminary round is representative of the overall tournament strength.

The average preliminary round will include six or seven fencers, three or four of whom will qualify to advance to the second or semifinal round. The semifinalists then compete to earn advancement to the final round, which will include no less than six contestants. The fencer who wins the most bouts in the final round is declared the winner of the tournament. In the event of ties for first place, a fence-off or *barrage* is held in which the tied fencers compete again to determine a winner. When there are ties for second place or less, a barrage is not fenced. Placement is determined according to "indicators," which is the ratio between touches given and touches received during the entire final round of competition. In effect, while the fencers are tied on bout scores, it is the fencer who has received the fewest touches and who has delivered the most touches who will be placed higher when indicators are computed.

TEAM TOURNAMENTS

Team tournaments are normally fenced as complete round-robin events, unless an unusually large number of entries makes it practical to resort to elimination rounds. Teams are composed of three fencers plus an alternate, who may substitute for a team member in the event of injury. When fencing as a team, each member must fence each team member of the opposing team. The team winning the majority of bouts in a given team match is the winner. Nine bouts are fenced in a single team match, so a team need win only five bouts for a winning score. However, it is important that as many bouts be won as possible per team match in the event of a tournament tie. When teams are tied on match scores, the team which has won the most individual bouts during the tournament is declared the winner. If a tie still exists, the team which has received the fewest touches is declared the winner. If there is still a tie, touches given are counted to determine a winner. If, through some miracle, a tie still exists, the tied teams must fence a barrage.

TOURNAMENT STRATEGY

The particular method an individual or team uses to approach tournament fencing can spell the difference between defeat and victory. For best success the fencer must formulate sound tournament habits which are conducive to maximum fencing concentration throughout the duration of a day's competition. All of one's energies should be directed to one end, and that is to fence at top performance in every single bout of the day. The fencer must remember that an average tournament will require one to fence approximately twenty bouts, any one of which the fencer can win or lose. In short, one fences for bout scores and not tournaments, and the fencer who is unprepared mentally or physically to sustain a concentrated effort from the first bout to the last will have little chance for best results. The following suggestions may serve as a guide for high-level tournament performance.

1. Service all fencing equipment the day prior to a given tournament. Check body cords, clean the foil button, and test its spring for proper resistance. Be sure that the metallic vest is free of tears or loose threads. Wash and iron the fencing uniform, making sure that all buttons, zippers, etc., are in place and working properly. Equipment problems must not be allowed to serve as distractions once the tournament begins. Few fencers appreciate the importance of this kind of careful preparation. It is a common occurrence in the fencing world to see fencers arrive at the tournament site, where they rush madly around making equipment adjustments at the last minute. One can hardly expect a good performance from a fencer who arrives unprepared, not knowing whether the equipment can successfully survive a day's competition. Proper preparation can be worth an extra touch per bout.

2. Arrive at the tournament site one hour before starting time. This hour is of crucial importance, for it gives the competitor ample time to meet old acquaintances, and to register. It also affords time to have one's weapons officially tested and cleared, and to warm up and rest before fencing begins. Warming up should include at least ten minutes of running, stretching, and lunging exercises. When this is completed, twenty minutes of light fencing with anyone available should be sufficient to complete the warm-up period. This sparring must *never* take on a competitive emphasis, but should be done soley to awaken the defensive and offensive systems of one's game. All competitive energy must be saved for the tournament, where it will be most needed.

3. Prior to the beginning of the tournament, all necessary fencing equipment should be placed where it can easily be located. After the bouting starts, if a foil should break or a body cord or vest need replacement, the fencer should be able to replace the necessary items quickly. Nothing must be allowed to break one's concentration once a bout has begun. It is most difficult to reestablish fencing concentration once it has been broken at the midpoint of a highly competitive bout.

4. Before the tournament and *prior to each bout*, ensure that the opponent's metallic vest is registering properly. If not, insist that it be changed. If one should find reason to question equipment during the bout, time must be taken to ensure that all is well. For example, if what appears to be a valid touch is made and a white light is activated, or if no light at all results, the weapon should be tested before resuming play. Testing one's foil against the opponent's metallic vest or against one's shoe (never the floor) after the director has given permission, will normally be sufficient. There is no psychologically advantageous time during the bout in which to repair weapons, for, again, concentration will be lost. When in doubt, change the equipment. The fencer cannot afford the psychological insecurity that is an inevitable result of equipment that isn't one-hundred-percent trustworthy.

5. Between bouts, always stay warm. A jacket, sweatsuit, blanket, or robe should be immediately available at the termination of every bout. The fencer must never allow himself or herself to cool down while waiting to fence again. "Going cold" is a common hazard in fencing and the careless fencer who does so will certainly be defeated when faced with a worthy opponent.

Fig. 13.1. Getting ready to fence.

6. Between bouts, the competitor should remain quiet and observant. This is the time in which information relating to one's competition may be gained, and used when one's turn comes around to fence again. Concentration is easily lost when friends, spouses, children, etc., insist upon conversation which is not related to the immediate circumstances. After the tournament is over there will be ample time for socializing.

7. When fencing, every effort must be made to defeat every opponent totally, without receiving touches against oneself. To ensure bout victories concentration must be on *touches* and not specifically on bouts. The bout score will always take care of itself. The margin by which one wins or loses is important, for in the event of bout score ties one may proceed to the next round on indicators. If one's bout score margins are wide on victories and narrow on defeats, one need not lose when indicators are computed.

8. When one has won enough bouts to ensure advancement to the next round, there is no longer a need to continue an all-out effort for the possible remainder of bouts to be fenced. It now becomes especially important to save as much energy as possible for the next elimination round where it will be needed even more. It is a common error among fencers to fence as hard for bout victories which are not needed as they did for those which were crucial. The fencer does well to remember that *the object of all preliminary rounds is to reach the finals and not necessarily to win every bout along the way.* The experienced fencer conserves energy, fencing only hard enough to ensure passage to the next round. This way, when one reaches the finals, one will be fresh and capable of an all-out effort for tournament victory. It is in the final round, where the fencing is the strongest, that every ounce of the fencer's remaining energy will be put to the severest test. The fencer must anticipate this time. It is most embarassing to reach the finals of a good tournament only to discover that in getting there one has "run out of gas." This is a common occurrence in fencing and one that is quite needless.

9. Keep an ear open to the director Every director has definite fencing preferences. Just as no two fencers fence alike, no two directors see all action in exactly the same way. The fencer does well to listen carefully to all analyses the director may make relative to any given fencing phrase. In this way, the fencer may learn how the director sees and interprets action, and may well

learn something which will improve his or her chances to score. The fencer who makes mistakes in timing and execution can always learn from the director where these errors reveal themselves.

Always fence for the director. If the director shows a preference for attacks, attack. If the director shows a preference for stop thrusts, stop thrust. Under no circumstances can the fencer allow himself or herself to continuously repeat actions which the director clearly does not acknowledge. If one does not agree with the director's decision, one may *politely* request that the action be analyzed for further clarification.

Many directors are relative beginners, like most of us, and will make honest mistakes from time to time. The experienced fencer will never allow a bad decision to disrupt concentration. Conversely, one must make every effort to score with clearer action next time. When fencing for an unfamiliar director, one would be well-advised to fence cleanly, with well-executed technique which displays knowledge of right-of-way, and with decisive action which scores well. If these points are observed, one need not worry about the director's visualization. A good fencer will, through the excellence of his fencing, be seen.

CHAPTER 14

THE FENCING PROGRAM

FACILITIES

One of the essential ingredients for a successful fencing class is space. Of course a gymnasium is excellent, but any large room with reasonably good lighting and adequate floor space will suffice. A wood floor is mandatory in order to spare students the discomfort of tired feet or shin splints. Convenient storage space for masks, gloves, foils, scoring equipment, etc., is always a blessing. If circumstances permit, lines should be painted or taped on the floor indicating the boundaries of one or more regulation fencing strips. Fencing without floor markings is not unlike playing tennis without indicated boundaries.

CLASSES AND EQUIPMENT

The ideal number of students per class should be twenty. While classes of over twenty can be managed, the teacher will experience, in proportion to increased numbers, greater frustration and instructional ineffectiveness. All first-year teaching should relate to group instruction, allowing individual lessons only to those who need extra help.

The equipment that will be needed for twenty students should make allowances for from one to five left-handed fencers. While a class may well be composed of only right-handed fencers, there are times when a rush of "lefties" will appear, and it is best to be prepared in advance. To equip a class of twenty students, the following list of equipment is mandatory for safety as well as instructional efficiency:

1. *Twenty-five French foils.* Of these, twenty should be right-handed and five left-handed. When purchasing foils, do not cut costs, for a good foil will last five times longer than an inexpensive model. An excellent class foil will include an extra heavy blade, a steel rolled-edged guard, and a leather-wrapped handle.

2. *Twenty French blades.* It would be convenient to have spare blades on hand especially when teaching beginners, who will be unavoidably insensitive to the amount of pressure it takes to score a valid "touch." A class of twenty can be expected to break ten or fifteen blades in a semester of instruction. Fortunately, blades are not too expensive.

3. *Twenty fencing masks.* The fencing mask is the most important safety feature for fencing. Any medium-priced foil mask will provide excellent service for several years.

4. *Twenty-five foil jackets.* A good fencing jacket is essential for safety and comfort. As with foils, it is best to include twenty jackets for right-handed fencers and five for the left-handed fencers. Where budgets are low, "half-jackets" will save money and are perfectly suitable for beginning instruction.

5. *Thirty fencing gloves.* It is wise to include extra gloves to allow flexibility in fitting for size. The majority of gloves should be medium in size, with a few small and large sizes to accomodate others. Include five or six left-handed gloves of assorted sizes. Most medium-priced gloves will give adequate protection and wear. Expensive gloves are priced more for their aesthetic value than for practicality.

6. *Thirty pairs of fencing knickers.* Students can usually supply their own trousers (hopefully white), for almost any cloth covering on the legs will give the necessary protection. However, it is advised to furnish fencing knickers which are designed for the stress of the lunge and offer more comfort. Fencing trousers are the most difficult items of fencing equipment to fit to class sizes. A wide assortment of sizes is helpful. Don't forget the left-hander!

7. *Ten lunging pads.* This final item of class equipment is the teacher's most helpful instructional aid. The lunging pad gives the beginning students their best opportunity to practice thrusts on their own time. Ideally, a class of twenty would have twenty lunging pads. However, wall space does not always allow for this luxury, and so it is recommended that as many lunging pads be provided as budgets and space will allow.

CURRICULUM

The ideal college fencing program will include beginning, intermediate, and advanced levels of instruction. The beginning class can impart only the basics and, if successful, will inspire the student to continue on to the intermediate class. At this level the student may work for improvement in his or her basic game, pick up new material and gain fencing confidence before moving on to the advanced class. The advanced class should be structured so the student may repeat it as long as he or she is in school. It is unwise and virtually impossible to combine beginning and advanced fencing within the same class, where large numbers are involved. Also, it must be observed that the designations of beginning, intermediate, and advanced are general terms for instructional convenience only. As in many sports, we must recognize that anyone who has fenced for less than two or three years is a relative beginner.

Instructional Objectives

Fencing experts agree that given excellent training conditions five years is the realistic projection for beginners to achieve sound competitive proficiency. In view of the relatively short time that the high-school or college teacher will work with any particular student, it becomes obvious that the teacher is confronted with a most difficult issue of teaching sound fundamentals, while keeping students interested in a very complex and demanding sport. Fencing technique, with its hundreds of alternative moves relating to attack, defense, distance, and timing, poses a difficult question. Just what is fundamental to the game and how does one teach it effectively?

Substantiating Basic Development

The surest path to meaningful instruction lies in simplification, clarity, and observable progress. The teacher must stress the basic issues involved in fencing movement. If the basics are not stressed, one is inclined to proceed into a labyrinth of fencing techniques leaving behind the essential foundation upon which all fencing progress depends—that of balanced movement and tactical judgment. If the beginning fencer can be instilled with efficient movement and lucid tactics, he or she is well on the road to an enjoyable and effective game.

Modern competitive fencing, with its increasing emphasis on timing and distance, demands that the performer first master body mechanics, which will reflect itself in more efficient movement. The fencer should be disciplined in a thorough understanding of techniques which specifically relate to movement. Faulty habits in controlled movement are the root causes for poor performance on all levels of fencing. The fencer who moves well will find little difficulty in mastering the technical and tactical facets of attack and defense so essential to a sound game.

Emphasis on Balance

Balance is the most essential element for fluid movement. The lunge, parries, ripostes, etc., are more easily understood when placed in a context where balance becomes the dividing point between defensive and offensive postures. While every defensive and offensive movement in fencing has its own total commitment, all action should initiate from, and end on, balance. Offensive and defensive movements should not interfere with each other. For example, when teaching the lunge, emphasis should be centered on the student's ability to recover back or forward to guard position. If the lunge is static, or if balance is lost, the recovery becomes cumbersome at best. The lunge is only as good as its recovery. Let us take one more example. When teaching defense it should be stressed that the parry is only as good as the scoring opportunity it creates. At the conclusion of a parry the fencer's hand should be relaxed and ready to riposte direct or indirect or not riposte at all. In this way the student is given the understanding and capability to riposte whenever, wherever, and however it best suits the circumstances.

This approach to teaching adds interest, understanding, and challenge to all practice. The student soon discovers that balance is a solid commodity which becomes the key to fencing effectiveness. Once this discovery is made, all technical explanations will begin to make genuine educational sense. It is recommended that all basic technique be taught as an expression of offensive and defensive balance. Taken from this perspective, the fencer will train to overcome the mental and physical inertia of his or her own body. This leads to a faster, better-controlled, sensitive, and more powerful scoring ability. The student discovers that he or she has gained new power because energy is not being wasted in a struggle with one's own body. Economy of movement enables the fencer to recover from the split-second mistakes that unavoidably result during the intense interaction of the fencing bout.

Balance drills. The student should be able to execute the advance, retreat, lunge, recovery (both forward and backward), advance lunge, pattinando, and ballestra without loss of balance. The class should be drilled regularly in these actions in a variety of combinations: extend advance; retreat on guard, retreat extend; advance on guard, advance, lunge, and recovery; retreat, lunge, and recovery; pattinando and recovery, etc. Here footwork and body posture become integrated. The possible combinations are infinite and limited only by the teacher's imagination. The goal of this type of work session is to develop the student's ability to move in any direction at any given moment. Weight should not be allowed to settle in either an offensive or defensive

Fig. 14.1. When balance is lost, anything can happen.

posture. This session can be made into a game where the instructor tries to trick the students into an off-balance situation. Students love it.

Additional Skills and Drill Times

When new techniques such as parries or attacks are introduced, they should be practiced in context with the body drill: guard in sixte, retreat in quarte; quarte guard, retreat in sixte; octave guard, retreat sixte, retreat quarte, riposte; sixte guard, attack, recover to quarte, riposte; attack with pattinando, forward recovery to quarte, retreat and lunge. The student will find that the combinations are inexhaustible. Variety and surprise in such combinations will create excellent student response. This type of training should become a routine part of all class meetings.

The duration of the drill depends on the instructional situation. It should never be less than ten minutes and seldom more than thirty minutes. This approach keeps the student in constant touch with fundamentals regardless of the introduction of new technique. It also helps the student correlate the relationships between technique and balance. When errors are made in the bouting situation, he or she can pinpoint them and make the proper corrections. Thus the student becomes his or her own best critic. Again, the most frequent mistakes made on all levels of fencing can be traced to poor balance and the resulting loss of technical control.

Entrenchment of "Right-of-Way"

A second major area of special emphasis for instruction exists within the general rules and regulations relating to tactical advantage. At the core of the tactical element lies the concept of right-of-way. Complete understanding of right-of-way and its relationship to fencing tempo is essential to the beginner if he or she is to develop good basic fencing habits both in thought processes and in physical movement.

In effect, the student who learns to move well and think perceptivly in his or her early training will have little difficulty in later development. At this stage the fencer will arrive at a point where he or she can not only plan the proper move, but also possess the capability to deliver it effortlessly and on time. He or she achieves the ability to compete without theory interfering with execution and without execution hampering theory. With this balanced foundation the young fencer will make maximum use of all additional techniques he or she acquires.

Where balance is the key to effective technique, right-of-way is its counterpart in strategy. The teacher who stresses these fundamentals will find the fencing program progressing more rapidly. Students will react with enthusiastic participation because they are experiencing the results of sound basic preparation.

TEACHING SUGGESTIONS

When teaching a skill sport, the progression in which materials are presented can contribute to teaching effectiveness. In this respect fencing presents its own special demands. For example, should the student be given a foil before or after the guard position and basic footwork have been established? Does one teach basic defense or offense first? Which parries are taught first? Which attack? Questions such as these do not lend themselves to clear-cut answers. Few fencing teachers completely agree on what the most effective course progression should be, or which aspect of fencing should be given first emphasis. The answer lies within each instructor's view of fencing and the kind of objectives one has in mind. For a recreationally oriented program, course progression may well center around the fun aspects of fencing, where materials may be presented in relation to student interest. Here the teacher may not particularly be interested in high-skill-level performance and may approach fencing in a relatively casual manner. On the other hand, the teacher may well place instructional emphasis on preparation for high-level performance, where fundamentals and course progression are of more importance.

It has been my experience that both the recreational and competitive goals of fencing can be satisfied through a single approach. It is with this view in mind that the teaching unit presented in this chapter has been arranged. While the material for this outline of course progression has been derived from teaching experience which extends over a period of years, it is intended to serve only as a general guide to instruction. Hopefully this unit will be useful as a reference with which one may improvise according to specific teaching interests and circumstances. The unit includes the *maximum* amount of material that one can reasonably be expected to teach in twenty one-hour class sessions. Also, it is my firm opinion that beginning instruction should emphasize fencing appreciation, where the student will learn a good deal more about fencing than can be performed after twenty hours of instruction. The student at this point should be enjoying a beginner's game, but, more importantly, he or she should be able to recognize and hopefully appreciate skilled performance. In this way the young fencer will have a knowledgeable basis upon which to decide whether or not to continue on to advanced training.

UNIT, INTRODUCTORY FOIL, TWENTY HOURS

Goals

To develop basic competence in, and appreciation of, basic modern French-Italian foil technique. Emphasis should be placed on:

1. Fencing as a physical and mental conditioner.
2. Fencing as a recreational sport.
3. Fencing as competition.

Meeting 1

1. General introduction to fencing as it exists in the United States; i.e., students are told where fencing exists, who fences, why they fence (fun and sport), and how fencing is organized. This includes a general explanation of the A.F.L.A., the F.I.E., and collegiate fencing.
2. Thumbnail sketch of the historic development of fencing with emphasis on the Italian and French schools. The process of how these schools have come together to form the modern "international" competitive technique should also be explained.

Meeting 2

1. Guard in sixte. Foot position, knee position, left arm position, sword arm position, and torso position.
2. Lecture on the rationale for the guard and how its components function.
3. The advance and retreat.

Meeting 3

1. Line drill, reviewing guard and footwork (fifteen minutes).
2. Extension (development) and return to guard in sixte.
3. Development and return to guard while advancing and retreating (extend — advance, retreat — on guard).
4. Lecture on the importance of footwork and its relationship to distance.

Meeting 4

1. Line drill and review (fifteen minutes).
2. General introduction to types of foil grips; i.e., French, Italian, Belgian, Spanish, American, and Levits.

3. Lecture on the advantages of the French foil for the beginner.
4. Introduction to the foil: pommel, handle, thumb pad, guard, blade (tang, strong, medium, weak, and point). Students receive foil, take it apart and reassemble it.
5. The grip and its relation to the forearm.
6. Line drill and review with foil in hand.

Meeting 5

1. Line drill and review with foil in hand (ten minutes).
2. Introduce the lunge and recovery while giving a complete explanation of the mechanics of the movements and how the lunge is used as a means of attack.
3. Review of development and its importance to the attack. "The hand precedes the foot."
4. Continued line-drill practice.
5. Discussion centering on physical conditioning. Sore muscles mean progress and are to be expected during the first few weeks of instruction. Hot baths are recommended.

Meeting 6

1. Line drill and review (five or ten minutes).
2. Line drill emphasizing correct lunging and good recoveries (thirty minutes including rest periods).
3. Each student lunges against instructor's target for the first feel of what a good touch is like.
4. Discussion.

Meeting 7

1. Line drill and review (twenty minutes).
2. Introduce partnership training. Students practice direct attacks to each other's high lines. They practice delivering well-executed straight action, feeling what it's like to hit and be hit.
3. Line drill and review.

Meeting 8

1. Line drill and review (five minutes).
2. Theory of the guard as it relates to the outside high line. Explanation of target area and its subdivisions.

3. Parry sixte (high line, outside).
4. Parry quarte (high line, inside).
5. Direct attack to inside high line.
6. Students pair off and practice lunging direct and parrying quarte and sixte.
7. Discussion (five to ten minutes).

Meeting 9

1. Line drill and review (ten minutes).
2. Introduce feints and beats. Lecture on methods of creating a threat to induce parry response.
3. Partnership training practicing direct and beat-direct attacks against partner's target and parries.
4. Partnership training practicing slow-motion feint disengages and beat disengages.
5. Discussion.

Meeting 10

1. Line drill and review (ten minutes).
2. Brief lecture on ground rules and how to spar.
3. Free sparring for the rest of the class. The fencing is expected to be rough and tumble, but it will be fun and exciting. Also, and more importantly, this experience will create lots of questions for the next meeting.
4. Brief discussion (five minutes).

Meeting 11

1. Line drill and review (ten minutes).
2. Discussion about reactions to last session's sparring.
3. Introduce rules of *right-of-way*.
4. Sparring for rest of session.

Meeting 12

1. Line drill and review (ten minutes).
2. Review beat and feint attacks.
3. Review parries.

4. Introduce the riposte. Discuss at length the need for a riposte to stop the jabbers.
5. Discuss proper sparring as it relates to practice.
6. Review right-of-way.
7. Sparring practice (perhaps five minutes).

Meeting 13

1. Line drill and review (fifteen minutes).
2. Introduce low-line parries.
3. Introduce direct attack to low line.
4. Partnership training practicing low-line parries.
5. Introduce feint attack to low line.
6. Sparring practice.

Meeting 14

1. Line drill and review (ten minutes).
2. Introduce the one-two (double disengage) as it is used after feints and beats.
3. Continued discussion of right-of-way and its importance to strategy.
4. Discussion of fencing "form" and the need for balanced and controlled action.
5. Students use remainder of time for either partnership training or sparring, whichever they choose.

Meeting 15

1. Free fencing or partnership training. Again, this is the students' choice (fifteen or twenty minutes).
2. Lecture and demonstration of directing and judging. Instructor directs while students judge and fence.
3. Discussion.

Meeting 16

1. Line drill and review (fifteen minutes).
2. Discussion and review of directing and judging.
3. Students form into groups and try directing and judging for themselves.

4. Question-and-answer period.

Meeting 17

1. Line drill and review.
2. Discussion relating to the necessity of parrying when attacked.
3. Discussion clarifying right-of-way as it relates to parries as opposed to the remise.
4. Introduction of stop thrusts. Careful attention given to the rationale for stopping action.
5. Instruction in the direct and indirect stop thrust. (This is best done in the line drill where students stop thrust on the instructor's signal.)

Meeting 18

1. Line drill and review of stop thrusts (ten minutes).
2. Instruction in the techniques and rationale of the passata-sotto, in quartata, and knee drop as means to defensive stopping action.
3. Sparring for remainder of time.

Meeting 19

1. Line drill and review of all material covered thus far (one hour).

Meeting 20

1. Line drill (five minutes).
2. Discussion (five minutes).
3. Free fencing!
4. Remind the students that the intermediate or advanced class awaits their arrival. Goodbye, and have a nice vacation.

INTERMEDIATE INSTRUCTION

The intermediate class provides the fencer with an environment in which the gains made during beginning instruction may be practiced and consolidated before moving on to advanced instruction. Intermediate instruction should stress the need for improvement in techniques already possessed by the student. Instruction may include line drills for conditioning, partnership training, ample experience at informal judging and directing, and lots of free time for sparring. The instructor should be free to observe students fencing, and to offer objective advice to individuals concerning specific techniques which need improvement.

New techniques should be introduced from time to time as students, through their progress, indicate they are ready for them. Students' interest and motivation are assured when they realize that continued progress will open new doors of tactical and technical speculation.

Informal round-robin tournaments are a most effective tool for teaching students to direct and judge. It also helps them become aware of the importance of right-of-way and form in fencing. All fencers love to officiate once confidence is developed through practice. The experience gained here leads automatically to better fencing and also creates interest for the class.

Special time must be given to discussion and instruction in the techniques of sparring. Students enjoy sparring, and improvements in sparring procedure create the kind of informal competitive interaction which is most enjoyable. The teacher should stress the need for courtesy and good sportsmanship where touches are readily acknowledged, and encourage students to practice specific technique as the prime objective of sparring.

Finally, the intermediate class should be low-pressured and centered on the development of fencing skill as a means to *recreational enjoyment*. Every student must be encouraged to improve at his or her own rate. The student who does not progress in some small way with each session will soon become bored. The slightest improvement in the fencer's skill will generate enthusiasm which far outstrips the available practice time. At the end of each class the students should feel they have worked hard and increased their understanding and skill.

ADVANCED INSTRUCTION

Advanced instruction has as its central objectives increased physical conditioning, advanced methodology, and instruction which relates to tournament participation for those students who wish to gain competitive experience. The advanced class may be structured essentially as an extension of intermediate fencing, where the line drill, partnership training, officiating, and sparring are the means to improvement. However, the line drills will be more demanding, working the student to near exhaustion with each session. Partnership training and sparring become more precise as advanced techniques are introduced. Students are encouraged to supplement class time with additional exercises such as jogging and wind sprints. The teacher may offer more specific attention through the individual hand lesson, encouraging highly motivated students to gain tournament experience as a means to improving fencing skill. Ample time should be given to discussions which relate to fencing theory and practice.

However, all instruction should be geared to the abilities of all of the students. Instruction must essentially prepare the fencer for fencing as a recreational means to health and enjoyment.

COACHING

Many teachers must also function in a coaching capacity, where competitive strength is geared specifically to the tournament situation. Only the most motivated fencers should be included in coaching sessions where the individual lesson becomes the primary means to instruction and training. The coach's responsibility is to perfect and polish the fencer's technical foundation, bringing the fencer up to the highest possible skill level. The individual lesson is designed to sharpen the fencer's reflex responses; to develop exacting point control; to develop increased speed and power through a greater variety of offensive means; and to focus the fencer's perception in relation to distance and timing. The individual lesson relates to methodology which is impossible to study through class training. A fifteen- or twenty-minute individual lesson will tax every resource of energy the fencer possesses, always pressing skill and endurance beyond one's normal level of achievement. This type of lesson leaves the fencer mentally exhausted, tired, and wet. An individual lesson from a competent fencing coach is one of the most exhilarating and rewarding experiences in fencing.

In addition, the coach provides for the fencer a training schedule which supplements normal fencing practice and lessons. This ensures maximum endurance, which enables the fencer to fence at his or her highest level throughout the long hours of tournament competition. The coach and fencer enjoy a uniquely close relationship within the context of competitive athletics, and it can safely be conjectured that this relationship will continue on a social basis for many years after the fencer has graduated from school. There are few sports where the coaching responsibility is so intimately connected to the personality of the athlete. As I stated earlier in this book, the associations gained through fencing may last a lifetime, and in no area of sport is this more evident than in the relationship between the fencing coach and the student.

GLOSSARY

GLOSSARY

Absence of blade — Blades that are not in contact.

Action on the blade — Any form of offensive blade contact.

Advance — A forward step toward one's opponent.

A.F.L.A. — Amateur Fencers' League of America.

Attack — Any offensive movement which gains right-of-way.

Ballestra — The combined techniques of the jump and lunge as a means to attack.

Barrage — A fence-off between fencers who have tied for first place which determines the winner of a tournament.

Beat — A sharp spanking action on the blade used as preparation to the attack.

Bell guard — The portion of the foil used as protection to the hand and for the implementation of parries.

Bind — A preparation for the attack which transfers the opponent's blade from one line to an opposite line.

Blade — The portion of the foil from its tip to the guard.

Body cord — In electrical fencing, the insulated wire that connects the foil to the electrical circuit of the scoring machine.

Bout — Formalized combat between two fencers.

Broken time — A break or momentary change in the normal tempo of the fencing bout.

Button — The flat tip of the foil.

Cadence — The rhythm or tempo of the fencing bout.

Cede — To partially give way or to yield as a means of defense against binding actions on the blade.

Central guard — A defensive foil position which centers itself between the horizontal and vertical lines of the target.

Change of engagement — To engage blades in a new line.

Closing the line — A defensive movement with the foil which protects a line from possible attack.

Close quarters — When two fencers are too close to continue the fencing phrase but can still wield their weapons.

Compound attack — An attack which prepares with one or more feints.

Compound riposte — A riposte which is preceded by one or more feints.

Corps-a-corps — When two fencers make guard or body contact.

Counterattack — A stop thrust or attack into the tempo of the opponent's offensive preparation.

Counter-parry — A parry which defends against a riposte.

Counter-riposte — An offensive action which follows instantly from a parry.

Counter-time — A second intention movement which draws the opponent's counter attack in preparation for a scoring action with a parry and riposte.

Coupé [cutover] — A preparation for attack which withdraws the foil blade up and over the tip of the defender's blade, scoring to an opposite line.

Covered — A parry position which closes the line.

Croisé — A preparation for attack which engages the opponent's blade, transferring it from a high- to a low-line position but not, as with the bind, carrying it diagonally across.

Cutting the line — A parry which does not follow the normal pattern of defense, but instead binds the opponent's blade from one line to another. Usually the result of an overreaction while parrying.

Derobement — A deceiving blade movement with an extended arm which avoids the opponent's attempt to beat, bind, or take the blade.

Development—An extension of the sword arm as it precedes the lunge as one continuous movement.

Direct—An attack or riposte which does not break tempo or change lines on the way to the target.

Director—The official who presides over the jury during a fencing bout.

Disarmed—When a fencer loses control of his or her weapon or drops it.

Disengage—A movement made with the foil blade during the preparation for attack which transfers the blade under the opponent's defense to an opposite line.

Distance—The space between two fencers at any time during the fencing bout.

Doublé—An attack which deceives by circular disengagements the defender's circular parry system.

Double disengage [one-two attack]—A preparation for attack which deceives the opponent's attempt to parry with two consecutive disengages.

Double touch—Both fencers are hit simultaneously without either of them having the advantage of right-of-way.

Engagement—When two blades are in contact.

Envelopment—An engagement of blades as a preparation to attack which carries the opponent's blade in a complete circle, returning to the original line of engagement.

False attack—Any offensive movement designed to give the opponent the impression that one is attacking.

Feint—A false attack with the blade which is designed to draw a defensive reaction from the opponent.

Fencing—The sport of swordsmanship as it is carried out through regulations established by the Federation International d'Escrime and its affiliated organizations throughout the world.

Fence-off—See Barrage.

Fencing tempo—The time it takes to complete one fencing action. Tempo may vary according to the pace of a bout.

F.I.E.—Federation International d'Escrime. The official governing body for fencing throughout the world.

Field of play—The fencing ground or piste.

Finger manipulation—Method of controlling the foil by use of the fingers.

Fleché—A means for delivering an attack with a forward-springing action which employs a run for its recovery.

Foible—The weak and flexible portion of the blade comprising the third of the blade nearest the tip.

Foil—The weapon used for standard or electric foil fencing. Originally was the practice weapon for épée.

Forte—The strong and inflexible portion of the blade comprising the third of the blade nearest the guard.

Foul touch—An off-target touch.

Froissé—A powerful action against the opponent's blade designed to disarm.

Glide [graze]—A light action on the blade which exerts lateral pressure as it moves forward and which is designed to draw a parry response in preparation for the attack.

Gaining ground—Forcing the opponent back on the piste.

Grip—The means by which one holds the foil.

Ground rules—The regulations relating to the characteristics of the fencing strip, including the length, width, guard lines, and warning lines.

Grounding—The circuitry of electrical fencing which prevents touches from registering on the blade, guard, and fencing piste.

Guard position—The initial readiness stance assumed when fencing.

High lines—The lines of attack and defense above the fencer's foil blade, including the inside and outside high lines.

Hit—Any scoring touch to either the off or on target areas of the fencer.

Immediate—Any direct action which attempts to score.

Indirect—Any offensive action which attempts to score in the opposite line from that of the preparation.

Infighting—Fencing which continues at close quarters once the fencing phrase has been lost.

In line—Describes the point of the weapon when it is threatening the opponent's target.

In quartata—A side-stepping defensive movement which attempts to dodge the opponent's attack.

Inside lines — The lines of attack and defense to the left of the foil blade, including the high and low lines. (Reverse for the left-handed fencer.)

Insufficient parry — A parry which is too small or not strong enough to prevent an attack from scoring to its intended line.

Into tempo — A counterattack performed with a lunge which is executed upon the opponent's forward movement when preparing to attack.

Invalid touch — A scoring action which lands off target to the head, arms, or legs of the opponent.

Invitation — An opening in the defender's line, designed to tempt the opponent to attack.

Judge — One of four jurors who watch for touches in standard foil.

Jury — The officials (four judges and a director) who referee the fencing bout.

Lines — Theoretical lines of defense which divide the target area into four scoring areas, including the outside, inside, high, and low lines.

Lunge — The primary means by which the fencer delivers the attack.

Manipulators — The thumb and index finger, which guide the movements of the foil blade.

Meet — Fencing tournament.

Metallic vest — The lamé jacket which covers the target area in electrical fencing and which completes the circuit to register a valid touch in electrical fencing.

Mobility — Movements on the fencing ground which give or take distance.

N.C.A.A. — National Collegiate Athletic Association.

N.F.C.A.A. — National Fencing Coaches' Association of America.

N.I.F.A. — National Intercollegiate Fencing Association.

N.I.W.F.A. — National Intercollegiate Women's Fencing Association.

Off target — A hit which lands off the valid target surface.

One-two — Deception of the opponent's attempt to parry by use of two disengages.

Opposition — Control of the opponent's blade by means of pressure during either the attack or riposte.

Orthopedic grip — A handle designed to fit the contours of one's hand.

Outside line — The lines of attack and defense to the right of the foil blade, including high and low lines. (Reverse for left-handed fencer.)

Parry—A defensive movement with the foil which deflects the opponent's blade from reaching the target.

Passata-sotto—A classical ducking action which evades the attack.

Passé—An attack which slides by the target, failing to score.

Phrase d'armes—A continuous sequence of fencing action.

Piste—The field of play or fencing ground.

Pommel—The specially designed nut which is attached to the tang of the blade, holding the foil components together and lending balance to the weapon.

Point pressure—The 500+ grams of pressure required to depress the foil button for a scoring touch in electrical fencing.

Point travel—The distance the button must travel to complete the circuit for a scoring touch. May not exceed one mm.

Pool—The grouping of fencers who fence for advancement to a succeeding round.

Preparation of attack—Any movement of the blade, body, or feet which creates the scoring opportunity.

President—A synonymous term for director.

Press—Action on the opponent's blade designed to create an opening for attack.

Prise de fer—Taking or binding the opponent's blade.

Pronation—The sword hand when it is positioned with the fingers down and the back of the hand up.

Recovery—The movement which returns one to the guard.

Redoublement—An instant renewal of the attack performed with one or more preparations such as a beat, feint, or disengage.

Remise—An instant renewal of attack which replaces the point in the line of the original attack.

Reprise—The immediate renewal of attack performed after one has returned to guard.

Retreat—A backward stepping movement away from the opponent.

Rhythm—The pace or tempo established by the fencer.

Right-of-way—A scoring advantage related to timing which is gained by the fencer who first initiates an attack or who ripostes direct and without hesitation after a parry.

Riposte — A counterattack immediately following a parry.

Salle d'arms — A facility especially designed for fencing. The fencing room.

Salute — A gesture of readiness which acknowledges one's opponent before the fencing bout begins.

Second intention — A strategy of the fencer who is thinking a movement ahead of his or her opponent which may draw the opponent into a trap, creating an opportunity to score on a secondary movement such as a riposte.

Seeding — The ranking of fencers in preliminary pools according to individual fencing strength.

Semicircular parry — Combined parries which describe a half-circle motion from high to low line or vice versa.

Simple attack — Any attack performed in one tempo.

Simultaneous action — When both fencers attack with equal advantage of right-of-way.

Stop thrust — A counterattack performed by extending the arm as a means of scoring into the opponent's offensive preparation.

Straight attack — Any direct action.

Strip — The piste or fencing ground.

Supination — The sword hand when the fingers are turned up with the back of the hand facing downward.

Target — The torso of the body, including the front, sides, and back, which defines the valid surface for scoring.

Tempo — See Fencing tempo or Rhythm.

Thrust — Any action which conveys danger to the opponent's target.

Time thrust — A stop thrust which is designed to score while concomitantly deflecting the attacking blade from the target.

Timing — The most advantageous moment to attack which catches the opponent unprepared for defensive capability.

Troumpement — Evasive movements during the attack which evade the opponent's attempt to parry.

Warning lines — The lines drawn one meter from the ends of the piste. The fencer who retreats to this point is warned that the limit of the ground is being reached.

Yielding parry — Giving way to an opponent's binding action on the blade with the intention of gaining a parry.

SELECTED READINGS

SELECTED READINGS

ANDERSON, Bob, ALL ABOUT FENCING. New York: Arco Publishing Company, 1970.
A well-written book on fundamental foil technique featuring flip-page sequence photographs.

ANGELO, Domenico and Henry, THE SCHOOL OF FENCING. Land's End Press, 1971.
An excellent book for the history buff. Includes facsimiles of three rare and valuable books on fencing by the noted eighteenth-century fencing masters, Domenico and Henry Angelo.

BACON, Francis, THE CHARGE TOUCHING DUELS. New York: Da Capo Press, 1968.

BALDICK, Robert, THE DUEL—A HISTORY OF DUELING. New York: Clarkson N. Potter, Inc., 1965.

BOWER, Muriel and FARSO, Mari, FENCING, 2nd ed. Dubuque, Iowa: William C. Brown Co., 1972.
A most valuable handbook, which can be used to supplement instruction.

CASTELLO, Julio Martinez, THE THEORY AND PRACTICE OF FENCING. New York, London: Charles Scribner's Sons, 1933.
A book on foil, épée, and sabre fencing written by one of America's first and foremost fencing masters. A must for every fencer's library.

CASTELLO, Hugo and James, FENCING. New York: Ronald Press, 1962.
A first-rate book on modern fencing, beautifully photographed and including methodology for both the standard and electrical foil.

CROSNIER, Roger, FENCING WITH THE FOIL. London: Faber and Faber, 1951.
An excellent book for students and teachers alike.

CROSNIER, Roger, FENCING WITH THE ELECTRIC FOIL. New York: A. S. Barnes and Company, 1961.
Includes valuable material for tournament fencing and the electrical foil.

DE BEAUMONT, C.L., FENCING—ANCIENT AND MODERN SPORT. New York: A. S. Barnes and Company, 1960.
Includes a comprehensive treatment of foil, épée, and sabre. Well written.

DELADRIER, Clovis, MODERN FENCING. Menasha, Wisconsin: George Banta Co., Inc., 1954.
A comprehensive study of foil, épée, and sabre. Includes teaching methodology.

LUKOVICH, Istvan, ELECTRIC FOIL FENCING. Corvina Press, 1971. (Distributed in the United States by Sportshelf, P.O. Box 634, New Rochelle, N.Y. 10802.)
An excellent book relating to modern electrical fencing.

MOODY, Dorothy and HOEPNER, Barbara, FENCING FUN AND FUNDAMENTALS. Oakland, California: B & D Publications, 1971.
A comprehensive handbook on fencing especially designed for the teacher.

NADI, Aldo, ON FENCING. New York: G. P. Putnam's Sons, 1943.
This is perhaps the best-written book on standard foil fencing. It is comprehensive, relating to technique and bouting strategy, and offers the reader a view of fencing through the eyes of one of the world's greatest fencing professionals. A truly fascinating work of fencing literature and a must for anyone interested in fencing.

PALFFY-ALPAR, Julius, SWORD AND MASQUE. Philadelphia: F. A. Davis Company, 1967.
Includes methodology of the foil, épée, and sabre as well as an excellent and comprehensive history of fencing, and a chapter on theatrical fencing.

SENAC, Regis and Louis, THE ART OF FENCING. New York: American Sports Publishing Company, 1915.
The first book on foil fencing published in the United States. Very interesting from a historic viewpoint.

RULES BOOKS

AMERICAN ASSOCIATION FOR HEALTH, PHYSICAL EDUCATION AND RECREATION, FENCING-BOWLING GUIDE. Washington: American

Association for Health, Physical Education and Recreation. Published every two years. 1921 16th St. NW, Washington, D.C. 20036.

AMATEUR FENCERS' LEAGUE OF AMERICA, FENCING RULES. Westfield, New Jersey: Amateur Fencers' League of America, Inc. 1974.

NATIONAL COLLEGIATE ATHLETIC ASSOCIATION, THE OFFICIAL FENCING GUIDE. New York: National Collegiate Athletic Association. College Athletic Publishing Service, 349 E. Thomas Rd., Phoenix, Arizona 85012.

MAGAZINES

AMERICAN FENCING. Amateur Fencers' League of America, 249 Eton Place, Westfield, New Jersey 97090. Bi-monthly.

THE SWORDMASTER. National Fencing Coaches' Association, 16 No. Carrol St., Madison, Wisconsin, Quarterly.

FILMS

MODERN FOIL TECHNIQUES. 8mm. color film loops by Charles A. Selberg. Includes twenty loops of instructional film covering all basic techniques of modern foil fencing. Excellent quality. Complete study guide included. Purchase at American Fencers' Supply, 2122 Fillmore Street, San Francisco, California.

INSTRUCTIONAL FOIL. 16mm. black and white film by Julio M. Castello. The film includes a basic fencing lesson showing close-ups and slow-motion sequences. Purchase or rent from Castello Fencing Equipment Company, 30 E. 10th St., New York, New York 10003.

FOIL FUNDAMENTALS. 16mm. black and white film. Includes the guard, footwork, attacks, and defenses. Purchase or rent from the Amateur Fencers' League of America, 249 Eton Place, Westfield, New Jersey 07090.

OMNIBUS. 16mm. black and white sound film. Excellent film for the beginner. Purchase or rent from Amateur Fencers' League of America, 249 Eton Place, Westfield, New Jersey 07090.

FENCING—1964 OLYMPICS—TOKYO. 16mm. black and white film. Includes training and techniques of world's outstanding fencers. Rental only from Amateur Fencers' League of America, 249 Eton Place, Westfield, New Jersey 07090.

TECHNIQUES OF FOIL FENCING. 16mm. black and white film. Includes Helene Mayer, former Women's World Champion, demonstrating foil techniques. Purchase or rent from The University of California Extension Film Center, 2223 Fulton St., Berkeley, California 94720.

BEGINNING FENCING. 35mm. film strips in color with sound recordings by Maxwell Garret. Includes offensive and defensive strategies. Purchase or rent from the Athletic Institute, 805 Merchandise Mart, Chicago, Illinois 60654.

BASIC TRAINING OF FOIL FENCING. 16mm. black and white sound film by Hungarian Fencing Masters. Includes basic fundamentals of foil fencing. Purchase or rent from the University of California Extension Film Center, 2223 Fulton St., Berkeley, California 94720.

INDEX

INDEX